# THE MOUNTAINS WITHIN ME

by

## Zell Miller

Cherokee Publishing Company
Atlanta, Georgia
1985

**Library of Congress Cataloging-in-Publication Data**

Miller, Zell, 1932-
    The mountains within me.

    Reprint. Originally published; Toccoa, Ga.:
Commercial Printing Co., c1976. With new introd.
    Includes index.
    1. Mountain life — Georgia — History — 20th century. 2. Georgia —
Social life and customs. 3. Miller, Zell, 1932 - 4. Georgia — Biography, I.
Title. F291.M55 1985        975.8'04        85-19068
ISBN 0-87797-116-1 (pbk.)

This book is printed on acid-free paper which conforms to the American
National Standard Z39.48-1984 *Permanence of Paper for Printed Library
Materials.* Paper that conforms to this standard's requirements for pH,
alkaline reserve and freedom from groundwood is anticipated to last several
hundred years without significant deterioration under normal library use and
storage conditions. ∞

Manufactured in the United States of America

ISBN: 0-87797-116-1

 Cherokee Publishing Company is an operating division of the
Larlin Corporation, P. O. Box 1523, Marietta, GA 30061

Cover photo courtesy of John Jones Photography, Cornelia, GA.

For:

Birdie Bryan Miller,
    who made it possible

Edna Herren,
    who showed me the way

Shirley Carver Miller,
    who held my hand

Family, Relatives and Friends,
    who were with me in the mountains.

Contents

# Foreword

*Here is perhaps the most splendidly striking mountain scenery upon the face of the globe—an amphitheatre of probably 50 miles in circuit is formed by the Brasstown mountains and encircling a beautiful and fertile valley about four miles across, interspersed with limpid streams and making upon the whole a picture unsurpassed and rarely if ever to be equaled for the wildness and grandeur of its scenery.*

*Cherokee Indian Valuations of 1836*
John Shaw and George Kellog

That description of the valley where I was born and grew up is still an accurate one. The physical appearance of the valley is now dotted with homes, roads and electric lines, but the breathtaking beauty of the mountains has changed very little.

There were few white men in the valley in 1836. John Bryson and Alton Kirby had come in a few years earlier. Today there are only a few hundred more—still some Brysons and Kirbys—but the population is still relatively sparse. It was in this scantily populated village that my hopes were lifted and my ability to cope was nurtured.

In his Pulitzer prize-winning book, *The Americans: The Democratic Experience*, Daniel Boorstin writes that life is "more graspable" in smaller places. One could find fewer places smaller than Young Harris in which "to grasp."

My roots run very deep in the mountains of North Georgia. My ancestors were among the first mountain settlers. They wanted freedom, real freedom, and these mountains gave them the ideal setting. They were fiercely independent; and one of the ironies of history is that while the cowboy, another type of frontiersman, has been glorified, the mountaineer, the first frontiersman, has been ridiculed and caricatured in the image of "Snuffy Smith."

The independence of the mountaineer developed into individualism, and this personality trait, more than any other, is what has made people think us to be a little peculiar.

I am extremely proud of my heritage. I love the mountains in a way that is difficult to describe but that I hope will show through in the following pages. They are still where I can find my greatest solace and comfort, and my desire is to return one day, live out the remainder of my life and be buried in that valley that Shaw and Kellog described in 1836. "I will lift up mine eyes unto the hills. . . ." (Psalms 121:1)

There have been many excellent books written about the mountains and their people. This effort probably will contribute little new material. It is not meant to be a scholarly treatise, nor is it an autobiography. It simply is a personalized account of my environment.

There are many persons to whom I am indebted for their assistance. I could not have found the time to collect my thoughts and sort them out on paper if it had not been for an extremely capable and experienced staff in my office; so I express appreciation to *all* of them. I also am grateful to Don Rhodes for his help in the music chapter and Sharon Thomason on food. I also gratefully acknowledge the help of Aunt Lannie Hunter, Uncle Fletcher and Aunt Fannie Mae Miller. Mrs. Wilma Myers of Young Harris College wrote an excellent thesis on dialect which I used extensively.

I am especially grateful to Miss Edna Herren, who offered constructive criticism and still is placing commas in the right places as she did when I was in her English class at Young Harris College many years ago.

Marti Pingree, a fellow mountaineer, was of tremendous help and devoted many hours of her spare time to deciphering my scribbling on yellow legal pages. And much credit must go to Bill Burson, who offered many helpful suggestions and edited the entire manuscript.

And, of course, I am indebted to my favorite mountaineer, Shirley, who cheered the work on from beginning to end and, in a way, since Rail Cove is even smaller than Young Harris, served as chief technical adviser.

I

# Choestoe Kin

*Bring me men to match my mountains.*
*The Man From the Crowd*
Sam Walter Foxx

Only the most hardy and courageous settlers pushed over Frogtown Gap and into the rugged mountain country being vacated by the Indians after the land cession of 1835. Three centuries earlier, DeSoto, after spending some time in an area called Couchi by the Spaniards, decided against crossing these mountains and veered to the Southeast. Gold had been discovered in 1828, bringing explorers and prospectors into the Nacoochee Valley and nearby Araria. But these two locations were at the foothills, not in the craggy mountains farther north.

In December 1832, an area of 319 square miles was carved out of Cherokee country. John Thomas, whose descendants are one of the prominent families in this area, when asked what this new county should be named by the Legislature, replied: "Union, for none but Union men reside in it."

Slavery had not yet become the controversial issue it was to be a few years later. But there was a sharp conflict over the tariff, and President Andrew Jackson, whom these frontiersmen admired, had drawn the line between sectional interests and Union loyalty. "Old Hickory" had said in a famous toast, "To our Union, it must be preserved." Most Georgians thought differently and sided with South Carolina's John C. Calhoun, who had answered: "To our Union, after our liberties most dear." He then resigned as Jackson's Vice President.

This same degree of loyalty to the Union was to exert itself in 1861 even stronger when these mountain counties opposed secession.

Blairsville, the county seat, was incorporated in 1835 and was named for one of Andrew Jackson's allies, Francis Preston Blair, Sr., who established *The Washington Globe* to promote Jackson's reelection. The Blair House in Washington, D. C., also is named for this stalwart Jackson defender.

Indian history abounds in this area. Blood Mountain looms to the west of Frogtown Gap. An imposing mountain of 4,458 feet, it is the second highest in Georgia. Legend has it that an Indian war was fought between the Cherokee and the Creek nations on its heights and the next mountain westward. It raged so viciously that the mountains were named Blood and Slaughter. Between the two is Slaughter Gap.

As a settler crossed Frogtown Gap, which was renamed Neels Gap in the 1920's, the steep seven-mile mountain incline carried him into a valley the Indians had called "Choestoe" which was their word for "Land of the Dancing Rabbits."

There were three main ways into this wilderness. One could travel the Unicoi Turnpike, an old toll road built about 1812, which followed a Cherokee Indian trail of ancient origin. Unicoi is an Indian word for "New Way." Another was Tesnatee Gap, Cherokee for "Turkey," and the third was Walasiyi or Frogtown Gap. Walasiyi was the legendary great frog of the Cherokees that could hop across mountains.

It was in this valley that Jane Melinda Collins, my grandmother, was born in 1861.

Her grandfather, Thompson Collins, was one of the first white men to settle in this area, having moved some time in the early 1830's. He came from Buncombe County, North Carolina, where there is a record of a land transaction he made on the French Broad River in 1809. He lived in Habersham County while waiting for this new Indian country to be opened to settlers.

He died in 1858 and is buried in the old Choestoe Cemetery. He had brought his family of ten with him. Francis (Frank) Collins, my great-grandfather, was born in 1816 and was, therefore, a teenager when the family moved to Choestoe. Later, he and his wife also had ten children, and the next-to-the-baby, Jane Melinda, was born on July 3, 1861.

In 1886 she married William J. ("Bud") Miller, a native of White County, who had come across the steep mountain from White County several years before as a young school teacher. "Bud" Miller's first wife, Florence Edmundsin, had died a few years earlier leaving six children to rear. Jane was 24 years old; Bud was 38. They had nine children, making fifteen in all.

My Grandfather Miller's parents were natives of the Mossy Creek section of White County. Although the records are skimpy, we know that his father was James Miller, who was born the same year as my other great-grandfather, Frank Collins, in 1816.

At eighteen, James married Lydia Dunigan in 1834 when she was only sixteen years old. There were five children, of which "Bud" was the second.

Grandmother Jane Collins was from one of the oldest families in Union County and was considered almost an old maid. Her father had been the only school teacher in the community for several years. Her older brother, Francis Jasper ("Bud") Collins, was a merchant, farmer and cattle trader of note. He was known to have made 5,000 gallons of sorghum syrup annually and served in the Georgia General Assembly.

He never owned or wore a store-bought suit or ready-

made socks but preferred his homespun suits and hand-
knitted socks. An early account of this man reads: "He
was a man of great humility and of impeccable character."
I have a picture of Uncle "Bud," who had the same eyes
and facial characteristics of my father and his brothers
and sisters.

Another brother, Thompson Collins, or Uncle "Tomp"
as he was known, was one of the most loved men in Choestoe and one of its most interesting characters. His generosity and love for his fellowman are recalled to this day. It
was a well-earned reputation and came not only from the
blood that flowed in his veins but also from a very unusual experience as a young man.

Once, about 1875, two men he knew came to
"Tomp's" house and offered to hire him to take his mules
and pull their loaded wagon to the top of Tesnatee Gap.
Their mules just weren't up to such a haul. The bargain
was struck and "Tomp" hitched his team up and the three
started out.

Before they reached the Gap, Federal Revenue Agents
suddenly appeared in the road. The two men jumped off
the wagon and ran into the woods. The wagon was loaded
with moonshine liquor, and the agents offered not to make
charges against "Tomp" if he would tell them the others'
names. His response was "Never."

Thompson Collins was charged with possessing "un-
stamped barrels" and sent to New York to prison. A
couple of years went by, and the family did not hear from
him. Many thought he was dead. Then one day he came
walking into his front yard in Choestoe. He had walked
every step of the way from New York. He told his wife,
"I've slept in many a fence corner and cut many a stick of
wood for food. If ever a stranger comes by he is welcome
to sleep in our house and share my food."

He lived that credo and stories are still told of him.
Once, he was plowing in the field and a neighbor came and
asked to borrow his mule, meaning when he got through.
"Tomp" said, "Wait until I get to the end of this row."

Another time, at the mill, someone asked for some meal. "Tomp," who had just had his last bucket of corn ground, gave him his meal, slung his empty sack over his saddle horn and went and bought a bushel for himself.

My grand Uncle "Tomp" died in 1917 and is buried in Choestoe Cemetery. On his tombstone is chiseled "A poor man's friend." I hope I have some of my Uncle "Tomp" in me.

The claim has been made, and no one ever has disputed it, that Choestoe had a higher percentage of college graduates than any other rural section of America.

It would be impossible to list even the most eminent, but a partial list would include: Henry Duckworth and Charles Reid, both Chief Justices of the Georgia Supreme Court; Judge Bascomb Dever of the United States District Court; Dr. Joseph Henson, head of the Mathematics Department at Duke University; Dr. Jack Lance, F. M. Hunter, Stephen Grady Miller and Verdie Miller, teachers at Young Harris College; Byron Herbert Reece and many, many others including outstanding preachers like Tom Coke Hughes, the circuit rider known as "Bishop of the Mountains"; Marvin, John and Walter Twiggs; Jack Shuler; John Samuel Lance; Charles Rich; John Jarard; John Gilreath and Alfred Swanson.

One of the most famous was the grand old man of Georgia education, Dr. M. D. Collins, who was State School Superintendent for more than a quarter century. He was the son of my grandmother's brother, or my father's cousin.

No one can fully explain this phenomenon of an isolated mountain valley's producing so many distinguished lawyers, educators and influential citizens. Certainly heritage had something to do with it.

A Choestoe teacher, Frank Lloyd, has written that it was a combination of "talent, climate and blood." And Cecil Cobb Wesley has written: "Clannishness might have played a part in the success of Choestoens. If one attained a position of prestige, he helped his neighbors. But undoubtedly the strongest influence at work was the churches. Religion and education were almost one and the same." He mentioned one layman, "Bud" Miller, Sunday School superintendent at Salem Methodist Church, who encouraged young people "to participate in church programs and develop their speaking ability."

"Bud" was my grandfather.

He came to Choestoe to teach school. At that time anyone who could pass an examination given by the county school superintendent was licensed to teach, and he taught for a decade, mostly during the 1880's.

There were no official grades when he began teaching. The pupils were classified according to the level of their reading ability, and one was said to be in the first reader, second reader, etc. Students read aloud in class and learned their ABC's and multiplication tables.

The reading materials contained selections with moral lessons such as "Drunkards are worthless fellows" and "Love for trifling amusement is derogatory to the Christian character."

School did not begin until the corn had been "laid by" or plowed for the last time. It continued until fodder-pulling time. In a schedule by months this usually was from the middle of July to the middle of September. Later it was lengthened from "crop to crop" or from harvest time to planting time.

Some students had paper tablets and pencils that their parents had cut in half. Others had slates which cost 15 cents and were prized possessions. The student marked on it with a slate pencil and erased by spitting on it and rubbing it with the palm of his hand. There was a blackboard in my grandfather's school, and a piece of sheepskin was used for an eraser. There were no desks, only hard homemade benches.

A teacher was highly respected and my grandfather was no exception. His views were asked in politics and important matters. He was paid about $20.00 a month for about two months each year.

During the rest of the year he farmed, started a country store, and for more than a quarter of a century was Sunday School Superintendent of Salem Methodist Church, which, along with Old Liberty Baptist, was one of the most influential centers in the whole valley. In fact, for a number of years school was held in the churches.

My grandfather did not miss a Sunday for thirty years. The Sunday ritual began by his getting up and feeding the stock, putting on Sunday-go-to-meeting clothes and traveling three miles over muddy roads to Salem. The two youngest children would ride on the mule with him: one in front and one behind. The older children would walk and follow along.

Not only was it three miles to the church but one also had to ford the Nottley River. An old-timer remembers that as a child he went to Salem on a snowy Sunday morning. The wind was whipping off the frozen mountains, and the children who lived near the church were there and were saying, "I bet Uncle 'Bud' won't make it today," when they saw him coming across the river on his mule.

He had a mule that made a lot of noise when it drank water, and I have been told that when children made noise eating their food at a table their parents would reprimand them by saying, "You sound like Miller's mule."

Not only did he teach Sunday School but, like the teacher he was, he encouraged the young people to participate. He built a wooden platform in the grove nearby from which his students would deliver carefully memorized speeches.

With his large and growing family, $40.00 a year for teaching would not go very far; so "Bud" Miller turned more and more to running his country store.

It was a typical country store at the turn of the century. My grandmother ran it with the help of my father and his older brother, Dupree, after her husband died in 1919. Not an inch of space was wasted. It had large double doors, barred windows and the standard big front porch, but it did not have the Garrett Snuff and other signs usually found on country stores. It was painted green and a rock walkway led from it to the Miller home.

Inside there was "a little bit of everything" from plowstocks to drugs like Gray's ointment, turpentine, quinine, castor oil and "chill tonic." There were even ribbons and lace work which "Bud" always would call my grandmother to measure and cut.

A spool of rope hung overhead. My father learned as a boy that a mule and a plowstock were approximately 13 feet long and that 26 feet of rope would make a pair of lines. He also remembered a father bringing in a piece of string the length of the child's foot to get the proper shoe size. My grandfather knew by memory the sizes of all his regular customers.

It was hard and steady work. He dished up buckets of lard, weighed sugar and cut off salt pork. He assembled boxes of eggs which were sent on long trips to Gainesville by wagon loads.

This was a two-day trip and my father often drove the team of mules or accompanied other drivers. The wagons would be loaded with eggs, syrup, corn and animal hides.

The country storekeeper was also the resident philosopher. He knew every crop that was planted and every child born in the valley. He knew who would pay their debts and who would not. Paying one's debts on time gave customers high standing. Later as a boy, I always would go with my mother to pay her monthly bill because Leon would give her a free bar of candy for me.

Some of my uncles and aunts moved from Choestoe when I was a child. However, my Uncle Fletcher and Aunt Fannie Mae and many other relatives remained, and we visited them often. Each year a family reunion was held, usually at Vogel State Park or the Salem Church grounds, and Aunt Verdie, my father's sister, would take us in her car.

My grandfather's devotion to learning naturally extended to his own children. There was no high school or academy in Choestoe, but he was aware of Young Harris

College a few miles away and began to plan to send his children there. A very thrifty and proud man, he would not borrow money. However, he had made a loan to a neighbor and decided that the interest from it would be used solely to further his children's education. He called them in and explained that they could go one at a time "on the interest." They would go for a while until the money gave out and then would return home until more was available. When not attending, they worked in the fields, helped tend the store and taught in the schools in the valley. My father's first teaching experience was at Pinetop, a one-room school located at "the head of Stink Creek." He lived with his parents and rode there on a mule.

My mother, Birdie, wanted us to know first-hand how my father had traveled to Young Harris when he came as a student and how they later went back and forth to his home. The route from Young Harris to Choestoe is about eight miles through Trackrock Gap. I first walked it as a five-year-old and have both walked and ridden horseback through it many times since.

We always would stop to rest in the Gap itself at a nearby spring where there are the amazing boulders from which Trackrock Gap gets its name. The Cherokee Indians called it "Where There Are Tracks" and "Printed Place." No one is sure what caused the track-like indentures in the micaceous soapstone rock. Evidently they are of ancient origin and look like huge tracks of bear, opossum, raccoon and birds. One theory is that the Indians carved them in the rocks for their own amusement but, as a boy, I was told that live creatures left their prints in these rocks while the newly-created earth's surface was still soft.

One of my favorite Choestoens—long before he became famous—was Byron Herbert Reece.

"Hub," as we all called him, was tall and gaunt with hollow cheekbones and a shock of hair that, unless freshly combed, hung down on his forehead. He was a quiet and gentle person like most of my reticent relatives in Choestoe. He lived on Wolf Creek just down the mountain from where Vogel Lake now is.

For many years my Uncle Fletcher and his family were the Reeces' closest neighbors, and Aunt Fannie Mae remembers "Hub" coming to their house, after plowing a mule all day, and sitting on the floor and reading.

I would visit them often and was drawn to this intelligent and mild-mannered man. Once he discovered I was interested in insects and, on the next visit, gave me a book on *Insect Life*. He wrote in the flyleaf:

"Dear Zell: I hope this book won't outlast your interest in its subject, as it did mine. In any case it will acquaint you with the insect world, an interesting and varied world indeed. It sometimes is good for the human family to recall that if an insect had a fifth as much brain power as the human being we would have been vanquished long ago! Sincerely, Byron Herbert Reece, Jan. 6, 1946."

At this time of our lives, I was aware that he wrote poetry but was more impressed by his skill with a mule and his knowledge of nature and his intense devotion to protect the environment. Once when we were frog hunting in Vogel Lake, he made us pull the boat to the side of the bank to relieve ourselves. He explained, "We don't want to foul the water."

This remarkable man, who always declared that he was a farmer first and a poet second, was discovered in 1945 by the great author-poet Jesse Stuart from reading one of his poems in a magazine. Stuart wrote to him and offered encouragement, and in 1945 his first book of poetry, *Ballad of the Bones*, was published.

It received instant acclaim, and this mountain man was called out of the mountains to meet his public. Like so many of us, he found it very painful. There is homesickness and there is homesickness. But to a mountaineer, it is an excruciating feeling like an animal in a cage or a fish out of water.

But he was caught in a literary gale as numerous awards and invitations came his way. In 1950 his first novel, *Better a Dinner of Herbs*, won the Georgia Writers' Association Award for the best book of the year. Then rapidly followed *Bow Down in Jericho* (1951), *A Song of Joy* (1952) and *Season of Flesh* (1955). Poems appeared in such magazines as *Saturday Evening Post* and *American Mercury.* He won the coveted Guggenheim Fellowship and served as a distinguished lecturer at the University of California and Emory University.

Critics and reviewers acclaimed him. Jesse Stuart wrote: "He hasn't written just so many meaningless lines; but he has written lyrical ballads akin to the sixteenth and seventeenth century English and the early Irish poets. Here is someone speaking for the people of old American traditions. I think the *Ballad of the Rider* one of the best ballads by an American poet I have ever read."

Another literary critic, Marel Brown, has written, "In the year of his death he was crowding close upon the literary heels of Sidney Lanier."

In 1955, he published his last book, *The Hawk and the Sun*, and came back to teach at Young Harris College.

He was always frail and had spent time for treatment of tuberculosis at Battey Hospital, which was like a prison to this mountaineer.

One June night in 1958, he put one of his favorite pieces of music on a record player and shot himself. As a student at YHC he had written, "Death is an evil drum; Death is a country fiddler."

He was 40 years old at the time. He had created many lyrical lines, and there is no telling what could have come from this sensitive and gifted man.

> "Words that I have said,
> In accents sharp and muttered
> Are sorry things compared
> With those I never uttered."

On the side of Blood Mountain in a shady cove not far from his home in Wolf Creek, there is a monument to this Choestoen. One of his verses predicted his lasting fame:

"From chips and shards in idle times,
I made these stories, shaped these rhymes
May they engage some friendly tongue
When I am past the reach of song."

# II

# Young Harris College (1886-1932)

*Great things are done when men and mountains meet.*
*Gnomic Verses*
William Blake

Like honeysuckle in an old fence, Young Harris College and my life are inextricably interwoven.

I was born and reared in its shadow; both parents and an aunt taught in its classrooms; I attended both high school and college there and also served on its faculty.

It is a major part of what I was and am.

This mountain college, like many early educational institutions, had a humble beginning and was organized by a minister.

In 1885, the North Georgia Conference of the Methodist Church South assigned the Reverend Artemus Lester as circuit rider for the Blairsville Circuit. Part of his territory was Brasstown Valley in Towns County, an underprivileged area isolated from the rest of the state. Alfred W. Pierce, in *A History of Methodism in Georgia*, describes it as "very primitive."

Lester was reared in Monroe and Upson Counties. He entered the Methodist ministry in 1884, served one year at Lincolnton and then was assigned to the Blairsville Circuit. The officials evidently thought that such an assignment would not be too strenuous on one who was new, only 29 years old and unmarried. Although young, Lester was mature. His mother had died when he was 14, leaving him with many responsibilities, for he was the oldest of a family of ten children.

Lester was also a man of vision and ambition, and he conceived the idea of establishing a school in the settlement of McTyeire, which is now the town of Young Harris. This was quite a dream because as Pierce wrote in his *History*, "The people generally had received few advantages and the idea of a college education for their children had not yet become one of their aspirations."

Lester discussed his dream with the Reverend A. C. Thomas, Presiding Elder of the Dahlonega District. In many ways, it was unrealistic as there were only four families in the secluded mountain valley. However, Elder Thomas agreed and appointed the Reverend Marcus H. Edwards as first principal and sole faculty member.

A light-haired man with piercing eyes and a conservative mustache, Mark Edwards, from LaFayette, Georgia, was 38 years old. He had taught school three years before becoming a Methodist minister. Later, in 1890, he helped start Waleska Institute, which time evolved into Reinhardt College.

The new school was located in an abandoned storehouse in what is now the center of the town of Young Harris. An effort had been made to obtain land on the Union County line, where the College farm presently is located, but it was unsuccessful. Classes began in January, 1886, with three girls and four boys in the first class, all local citizens from Brasstown Valley.

During the spring of 1886, the financial needs of the new mountain school were made known to Methodists in the North Georgia Conference. Young Lofton Gerdine Harris, a leading layman of Athens, Georgia, responded to the request and contributed funds to complete the school year. It was the beginning of a lifetime interest in the mountain school, and without his assistance, the institution never would have survived. It is interesting to note that in spite of his loyalty and significant contributions, there is no record that Young Harris ever saw the school that later was to bear his name.

Young L. G. Harris, one of eleven children, was born in 1812 and spent his youth in Oconee County, Georgia. He studied law at the University of Georgia and was admitted to the Bar at the age of 22. He moved to Elbert County and was elected Representative in the Georgia General Assembly for several terms. He married Susan B. Allen, daughter of a wealthy Elberton planter, in 1835.

In 1840, he moved to Athens and again was elected to the Legislature from Clarke County. He also served as Judge of the City Court of Athens. He helped organize the Southern Mutual Life Insurance Company, which was founded in Macon, Georgia, in 1847 and later became president of the corporation.

Judge Harris also had an interest in religious activities, which grew out of his loyalty to the Methodist Church. He was superintendent of the Sunday School of Athens First Methodist Church for 40 years, served as a Steward of that church for many years and contributed liberally to its annual budget. He also donated funds for the construction of the First Methodist Church in Shanghai, China.

Through his work in the Methodist Church, Judge Harris learned of the newly founded school in Brasstown Valley. He and Mrs. Harris had no children, and he became interested in helping educate deserving boys and girls. Out of this interest in educating the underprivileged, it was only natural that he would respond to the request of Reverend Edwards for funds to help the school through its first year.

In 1887, the North Georgia Conference of the Methodist Episcopal Church South accepted the new institution as a conference school. By this time, the "Institute," as the new school was known, had an enrollment of 75 students and property valued at $3,000.

Since the Institute was a Methodist-affiliated school, it

was eligible to receive funds from the Methodist Church. It was expected to share in the training of ministers and to pronounce the Methodist faith in its academic activities.

In 1887, a charter was requested of the Towns County Superior Court:

> Your petitioners, to wit: . . . , desire to be incorporated under the name and style of Trustees of Young Harris Institute located in the state and county aforesaid at McTyeire on Brasstown, and the purpose of which is under the patronage, and is the property of the North Georgia Conference, M. E. Church, South. Wherefore they pray that they be incorporated as such trustees with the rights to receive donations, make purchases and affect alienations of property or personalty—not for the purposes of trade or profit but for promoting the general design of such institution and to look after the general interest of the same . . .

The Superior Court granted the charter on March 28, 1888. The school was officially named Young L. G. Harris Institute. As stated in the charter, its purpose was

> . . . the establishment, maintenance and operation of a college of Liberal Arts to give, promote and extend instruction and education in any and all branches of learning and education literary, mechanical, theological or otherwise as may be desired or deemed proper . . .

On July 25, 1888, the Young L. G. Harris Institute Board of Trustees held its first meeting in the principal's office on the Institute campus. Members present were these men who had petitioned for the charter: Chairman A. C. Thomas, Presiding Elder of the Dahlonega District; Methodist ministers W. F. Robinson and Edward A. Gray; Wier Boyd; B. W. Coleman; J. D. Cooley and Helm Hunt. Judge Young L. G. Harris did not attend the Board meeting, but a letter from him stating his views on the new Institute was read. Reverend Edwards, desiring to return to the active ministry, submitted his letter of resignation, and the Reverend Edward A. Gray, who had just become reassociated with the Conference after spending four years as a missionary to the Georgia Indians, was elected his successor as principal.

He was authorized to charge $1.00 per month for tuition. The Trustees also appointed a committee to investigate the property of the Institute and offer a report at the next day's session.

A part of the report read as follows:

> We find the land whereon the Institute is located is composed of sixty acres well selected in the beautiful valley of Brasstown in Towns County, Georgia—having all the advantages of good water, and attractive scenery, highly conducive to health and happiness.
>
> On this land there is already constructed eleven tenements, including the main building, mostly used and occupied as dormitories for students. The main building is well constructed, being sixty feet long, by forty feet wide; two stories high, with two rooms below and six rooms above, to which is added a dwelling house for Principal, a dining room and kitchen. These are well furnished with good spring water by iron pipes. We find a bell erected on a temporary structure, but a permanent one is in process of erection. A laundry is being fitted up with all the modern appointments of conveniences, etc.

In 1889, the Reverend C. C. Spence, a former cavalryman in the Confederate Army, was elected Principal, and the Board changed his title to that of President. A policy was adopted allowing school property to be leased to persons interested in "patronizing the Institute" and on which they could erect small houses where their sons and daughters could live while attending classes. (Some of these remained for many years, and my mother can remember a few still being located on the campus when she came there in 1919.)

In 1889, an attempt was made to move the new school to the nearby town of Blairsville. This was vetoed by the Board as was a similar proposal that the Institute unite with Hayesville College at Hayesville, North Carolina.

The Towns County Superior Court in 1891 approved an amendment to the charter empowering the Institute to confer diplomas. The first graduates of Young L. G. Harris College were Lala Simpson and Ida Stephens of McTyeire, W. S. Sanders of Danielsville, and Beulah Watkins of Gainesville. They received the A. B. Degree.

The mountain citizens of McTyeire were proud of their new college, and in 1892 received permission from the postal authorities to change the name of the village to Young Harris. The post office had been moved from near Trackrock Gap to about where it presently is located. The town of Young Harris was incorporated December 5, 1895.

Judge Harris donated 260 additional acres of land in 1892 and set aside $160 for the purchase of another tract of land near the school. In 1888, at a cost of approximately $5,000, he had constructed the first permanent building on the Young Harris College campus. It was a brick chapel erected in the memory of his wife and was to be used as a permanent place of worship for both students and community people. It was in this building, the Susan B. Harris Chapel, that I attended church as a child and where I joined the Methodist Church. It was where the funeral services for Dr. Joseph A. Sharp and my father were held.

Reverend Spence served as President until 1894 and then served churches in nearby White and Lumpkin Counties. Later, he established J. S. Green College in Demorest, Georgia, which later became Piedmont College.

Another Confederate Army veteran, the Reverend William F. Robinson, took his place and served for five years. He had been a member of the first Board.

Because of Robinson's leadership, the College not only survived but continued to grow and improve. Modern plumbing was installed in the girls' dormitory; all the buildings were covered with handmade shingles; and the great preacher, Sam P. Jones, accepted an invitation to speak at commencement. More than 2,000 people came from all over the mountain area to hear the speech which was made outdoors in a grove near where the present Clegg Building is located.

Judge Harris died during this period, and there was a great uncertainty as to whether the school could continue without this great benefactor who had made annual contributions to its operating costs. The general impression was that the school could not carry on without his assistance.

An estimate of the financial contributions of Judge Harris to the College would be difficult to determine because the institution kept no records of receipts or disbursements during the first two years of existence. During his lifetime, he gave funds for the purchase of approximately 400 acres of land and, upon his death in 1894, left the College 50 shares of capital stock in the Atlanta and West Point Railroad Company, 25 shares of capital stock in the Georgia Railroad and Banking Company and $5,000 in cash.

Though Judge Harris never visited the site of the college which bore his name, he made his views known through correspondence to its Board of Trustees. In a letter to the Board in 1890, he set forth his philosophy of the College in these words:

> I am for accommodating first of all the people in the section around our school. If we can do that and then have room for the regions beyond, very well, but first of all let us keep well in hand and in heart the interest of the people who live in that section of the state.

Dr. Jack Lance, a graduate of Young Harris College who later joined its faculty and then became its President, refers to Young L. G. Harris as the "Founder" of YHC and Dr. Joseph A. Sharp as its "Builder." That is an apt description. Dr. Sharp served two long periods as President. He was first transferred by the Conference to Young Harris in the summer of 1899, and he stayed until November 1916.

Born in Waleska, Georgia, in 1864, Dr. Sharp was a unique combination of preacher, teacher, farmer and businessman. An eloquent and moving orator who could quote not only the Bible but also Shakespeare liberally, he also was at home on the land. He had been reared on a farm before going to Emory University and knew what could be produced by the rich land of the mountain valley.

Therefore, the college farm was bought during his administration and used to make the college as self-supporting as possible.

Although a very persuasive man, he hated to beg for money and was reluctant to ask the Conference or churches for money.

Young Harris College was a four-year school until 1912. The debating societies flourished during this time, and students benefited as much from them as from classroom instruction. The Young Harris Society was organized in 1887, the second year of the school's existence. The Champion Debate was born shortly afterward, but in 1890, controversy and dissatisfaction resulted in one group withdrawing from the parent society and establishing the Phi Chi Society.

Leaders in this society split were Henry J. Fullbright, J. W. Prichett and Pat Haralson, and an intense rivalry was thus begun. The Phi Chis won the first debate; the Young Harris Society won the second and so on through every commencement until 1968 when the debates were discontinued. The Susan B. and Phi Delta Societies were organized for the young women.

After 17 years as President, Dr. Sharp was transferred to begin the Mission Training School and served the Wesley Memorial Church. He was given an honorary doctorate by the University of Georgia. Two years later he assumed the position of Headmaster of Emory University Academy at Oxford.

Another Emory graduate who had previously attended YHC succeeded Dr. Sharp as President. The Reverend G. L. King was a young man of 33 who had written numerous articles, including one with the provocative title of "Picking Pimples in Public." The Reverend J. L. Hall, like King, a native of Franklin County, became President in 1917. He was a very handsome man who also had attended YHC and had been a Champion Debater.

It was during Reverend Hall's administration that my parents came to YHC as teachers. My father had graduated from YHC and had then gone off to serve in World War I. He spent 18 months overseas, and his father had died before he returned.

In 1919 he returned to Young Harris College to teach history. His sister, my Aunt Verdie, also started teaching at that time.

In a professional education periodical in South Carolina, my mother had seen an advertisement for an art teacher at YHC, had applied and been accepted. She was to receive no salary but could recruit students at $2.00 a month, the same arrangement as for music teachers. She managed to recruit eight to ten students, which meant that she sometimes made as much as $20.00 a month. She roomed with Verdie Miller in the dormitory and ate in the college dining room.

My mother remembers that my father had only one suit of clothes and had to wear his Army uniform often during the first six months he taught.

Since it was too far to go home to South Carolina, she visited the Millers in their Choestoe home at Christmas. She remembers my grandmother stringing popcorn to go on the tree. Gradually, the friendship with Grady turned into romance.

After the first year, my mother had to return to South Carolina because her stepmother had died, leaving three small children who needed her care. My father had decided teaching did not pay enough for an aspiring husband and had gone into the jewelry store business with a friend in Gainesville. The venture did not work out, and he accepted a teaching job with his mentor, Dr. Sharp, at Oxford, and, persuading my mother to become his wife, took his new bride with him.

Neither Sharp nor Miller was happy at Oxford. They were mountain men and Young Harris College was in their blood. They were troubled by the news that YHC was not doing as well as it should.

A number of trustees, ex-students and others contacted Dr. Sharp and urged him to return as President. One Saturday afternoon during a card game of Rook, Dr. Sharp asked his former student and teaching colleague, "Grady, will you go back to YHC with me?" The answer was, "Of course, I will."

Dr. Sharp returned as President in May 1922 with Stephen Grady Miller as his Dean, and the next eight years were destined to be among YHC's finest.

An able faculty was assembled. William Lawson Peel, noted Atlanta banker and Chief of Staff for Governor Hoke Smith, became a major benefactor. Scott B. Appleby, who had been a student in the 1890's and had gone on to make a fortune, became interested in his Alma Mater. Large numbers of students from all over the South found their way to the mountain school. The debating societies flourished, and the farm produced milk, meat, grain and vegetables in abundance.

Dr. Sharp fulfilled the dream of Young L. G. Harris and Artemus Lester in making the College a place where the underprivileged mountain student could get an education. Many earned their way through college by working on the college farm or in the dining hall. Once, a grizzled mountaineer showed up outside the office of Dr. Sharp with a bull and swapped it for his son's tuition.

In March 1928, at the age of 66, Dr. Sharp became sick and died after a short illness. His funeral was one of the saddest occasions in Young Harris history. Students, townspeople and others filled the Susan B. Harris Chapel to capacity and spilled over onto the grounds outside.

For the remaining two months of the school year, Mrs. Sharp, the widow and a strong personality in her own right, served as acting president. Some felt Miller should be Dr. Sharp's successor; others favored Worth Sharp, Dr. Sharp's son, who was a teacher at YHC. Eventually, a decision was reached to go outside the present faculty, and Dr. T. J. Lance, father of banker Bert Lance, was brought back to the College as President. Jack Lance had been a student at YHC and had taught there from 1913 to 1916. He was serving as Superintendent of Schools in Waynesboro in 1930 when he came back to the College.

My father remained as Dean, and later Dr. Lance, under whom he served, wrote of him: "He did a magnificent piece of work for YHC. He was teacher, Dean and friend of students. His work of raising standards of scholarship was widely recognized." That is a fine tribute from a fellow educator and administrator.

Of course, I never knew my father, but the picture I get from many former students who have told me about him is of a gifted classroom instructor with a sense of humor who saw education not only as an intellectual exercise but a maturing process as well. "Stop messing with the side shows and come on under the main tent" was the way he sometimes put it to students.

Deeply interested in political affairs, my father ran for the State Senate in 1926 and was elected. He was aligned with his former YHC student, E. D. Rivers, who at that time was the President of the Senate and considered a progressive. Just as Dr. Sharp allowed my father to continue teaching while serving in the Senate, so President Charles Clegg, who was a student at YHC while my father was doing both, allowed me the same privilege 35 years later.

My parents had moved out of the dormitory to the Outlar House on a hill above the girls' dormitory for my sister's birth in 1926. Later they moved back into Hamby Hall and remained there for about five years until my mother was about five months pregnant with me. Then they moved into an old house on a hill near the campus where later the Blake Brysons were to live for many years.

One cold winter day, my father was handing wood through the window to my mother when suddenly he paused and asked, "Where would you bury me if I died?"

My mother, who had been present when Dr. Sharp had asked if my father would return to Young Harris with him, said: "Why, just as close to Dr. Sharp as I could get you."

My mother remembers a look of pleasure in his eyes and, without a word, he went back to carrying the wood.

A few months later, a sudden cold settled in my father's ear and developed into mastoiditis. On March 12, 1932, almost exactly two years after Dr. Sharp had died, Stephen Grady Miller passed away. He was 40 years old. My mother could not be with him on his death bed. I had been born in a drafty corner room 17 days earlier on February 24th.

Mother kept her promise. The Miller grave is within a few yards of where Dr. Sharp is buried on the hillside of Old Union Cemetery. A place is reserved for my mother next to him, and in the same plot his sister, my mother's roommate, Aunt Verdie Miller, is buried.

# III

# Growing Up in the Mountains

*Oh, would that I were a boy again,*
*When life seemed formed of sunny years,*
*And all the heart then knew of pain*
*Was wept away in transient tears!*

*Oh Would I Were a Boy Again*
Mark Lemon

Except for the almost three years we spent in Atlanta during World War II, my entire boyhood and youth were spent in Young Harris.

The young people with whom I grew up, like most from rural sections, scattered and now live in the cities and suburbs. But like filings to a magnet, most of us are drawn back to where we spent the days of our youth; and, on weekends and holidays, we often meet and compare notes on our jobs, our parents, our children and, for some, our grandchildren.

Memories come flooding back from these brief meetings—sweet memories of lazy summers and cold, sometimes vicious winters.

It is odd how one remembers the good and forgets the bad. Only my quirk about being warm remains from the unpleasant part, while the carefree days of my childhood seem like yesterday.

My earliest memories are of catching lightning bugs at night and butterflies during the day as they sipped nectar from the rows of thrift in our side yard. I noticed only recently that the very same kinds of butterflies briefly hover over the very same thrift 40 years later—which must say something about humans changing but butterflies remaining the same.

I remember falling in the three-foot-deep fish pond and being pulled out by Bill Bryson, who was awarded a safety pin as a medal.

I remember making and nailing to a telephone pole a sign reading "Pray for France" when the Germans were threatening and I had heard about it on the radio.

I remember how our lights would blink three times at night signaling that the electricity was about to go off from the power plant that generated electricity for the college and the community and how we lit the oil lamp that we used in the darkness that followed.

And I remember how when the river was dammed near Hiawassee, Lake Chatuge flooded Woods Grove, and the Tennessee Valley Authority brought us electricity 24 hours a day.

Soon afterward, Mother bought an electric refrigerator and stove on credit.

I had learned to read before I started to school at five years of age. It was a school that had four teachers: Mrs. Maude Potts taught the first grade; Miss Louise Waldroup, the second and third grades; Miss Bessie Howell, the fourth and fifth grades and Mr. Frank Erwin, who also was the Principal, the sixth and seventh grades.

The school was a wooden building in the same location as the present elementary school in Young Harris. Big sycamore trees with gnarled roots stood in front. It was a four-room school with a partition separating two of the rooms which could be opened for special events such as graduation and Christmas.

Heated by big, pot-bellied stoves, the school sat on stilts, and the wood used for heating was kept underneath the building. Each student was required to pay 75 cents a year for heat or his family could bring a load of wood. Boys in the sixth and seventh grades, strong and large enough to swing an ax, chopped the wood when the class was not being taught.

In the early days the students sat at double desks. One of my early seatmates was Bert Lance, son of the then-President of Young Harris College and now an Atlanta banker.

Graduation was a big event with the first and second honor students delivering carefully memorized speeches and with everyone else being presented in scholastic order. Mr. Erwin, a wonderfully sentimental man, always cried and had something good to say about each student.

The boys wore starched white shirts with their overalls, and the girls had ribbons in their hair. My sister remembers the kidding one girl got when it was noticed she had on a bra.

When I started to school my sister was in the seventh grade and was somewhat ashamed of having her younger brother tag along after her. Her greatest embarrassment occurred the first time I had to use the restroom at this strange place.

I held up my two fingers to get permission for "going"; but after walking down to the outdoor toilet and seeing that it was dirtier, wetter and scarier-looking than my own at home, I decided to go home. When I failed to return after an acceptable interval, Mrs. Potts, my first grade teacher, became apprehensive and sent someone to look for me. When I was not found, she reported my disappearance to the Principal, Mr. Erwin, who sent the big seventh-grade boys down to strike matches and see if I had fallen in. This mortified my sister when later it was discovered that I only had gone home to use the facilities there.

There was no water fountain, only a large bucket with a dipper. Each student brought his own glass or, in most cases, a small jelly jar. Boys were assigned one day a week

for carrying water from the well. The girls were responsible
for sweeping the room once a week.

There were no lunch rooms, cafeterias or canteens in
those days. During the lunch hour, those who lived close
enough to walk were permitted to go home. I lived close
enough, but preferred carrying my lunch like many of the
other students in order to have more time to play.

Lunches usually were carried in brown paper "pokes"
or lard buckets with holes punched in the lids to allow the
air to circulate. Students brought baked sweet potatoes,
sausage biscuits, boiled eggs and other such "delicacies."
"Light bread" with butter and sugar was a favorite of
those whose families could afford it. I often would take a
peanut butter sandwich and trade it for a sausage biscuit.

I also discovered that there was a great demand for
toothpaste sandwiches. My Uncle Vanus was a dentist in
Commerce and would give us small sample tubes of toothpaste. This, spread on bread like mayonnaise, was a real
treat for the mountain kids who did not have toothpaste at
home. I got a lot of good "swaps" that way.

I was in grammar school during the 1930's when the
school term was lengthened and free textbooks first dis-
tributed. Also from the "givernmint" students were given
surplus commodities like dried prunes, which no one liked
and all threw at each other, and hot chocolate mix, which
was served from big tubs.

Recesses were great fun.

We played "Red Rover," a game in which the participants lined up and held hands while the opposing side tried
to break through the line. If successful, the other side carried one opponent back and the process was repeated until
one side was completely depleted.

Drop-the-handkerchief, hop-scotch, skipping rope and
"dodge ball" were other popular activities.

Basketball was played on an outdoor court, and the
sixth and seventh grade boys and girls made road trips for
games to such far-away places as Brasstown and Hiawassee.
Mr. Erwin would load a dozen students into his '39 coupe

to make these trips, and those who went were filled with pride—and sometimes a little more.

Once we "city slickers" asked our rural neighbors at Gum Log where the "bathroom" was. They had no idea what we meant and there was a lot of ridicule about their ignorance. Actually, we were the dumb ones because we didn't know that outdoor toilets were not "bathrooms."

Sometimes after a "hog-killing" a student would bring a "hog bladder" to school. It would usually be almost as large as a basketball and we would play "Keep Away" with it. When the bladder began to lose air, we would put it by a hot stove and it would reinflate.

Shooting marbles was a big sport played for fun by the timid and for "keeps" by the more reckless. There were three different kinds of games—"bull's eye," "big circle" and "chase;" and, being one of the reckless ones, many days I went to school with a pocketful of marbles and returned home without any. After a few days a marble player's knuckles would become crusty and calloused.

A favorite game was "town ball." It was played with a rubber ball and a broomstick. You were out if you struck at the ball and the catcher caught it on first bounce or if you hit it and the fielder caught it on the first bounce. The most exciting way to be put out was by the pitcher's hitting the runner between bases with the ball. Some pitchers would try to hit the skirts of girl runners and make them fly up with resulting threats of "If you don't stop that, I'm going to tell the Principal."

"Root-a-peg" was popular also. This was played with a pocket knife and every boy had one. There were 15 to 20 intricate maneuvers by which the contestants tried to throw their knives and stick them in the ground. The winner then drove a matchstick into the ground as far as he could with three licks of his knife, and the loser literally had to root it out with his mouth.

"Swapping" knives was a pastime of all mountaineers which had its beginning in elementary school. One quickly learned there were some persons with whom you just didn't trade because of the high risk of getting the worst of the deal. My mother didn't like for me to swap knives, and before she would give me a quarter to buy one, she would make me promise solemnly not to swap it.

"Throwing" knives was a form of swapping that was even more risky. The throwers would grip their knives in their fists with only the jaws showing. Then each would hold his fist over the other's hand and when one said, "Let go," both would drop the knives.

Old automobile tires, or "casings" as we called them, were great playthings. When we could get them, we would roll them around with sticks while making sounds like racing automobiles. We would get them rolling fast, then jump astride and ride until spilled. The more daring would curl up inside and let someone push him down a hill.

Summers were great times, spent mostly on the banks of the creeks around Young Harris. We fished with poles, seined and set fish traps. The greatest fun was swimming in the places that to this day bring back memories of peace and tranquillity. There were Jackson Hole, Carson's Bottom, Sycamore, the Blue Bend and Cupid's Falls—all with their special diving places.

I have revisited these old swimming holes and have taken my children to see where their father spent so many enjoyable days during the hot mountain summers. But they all have changed. Some are now only knee-deep and the terrain has been altered by the growth and construction that have taken place during the intervening years.

The trips to the swimming places were adventures in themselves. To get to Sycamore, we went through a pasture where a new electric fence had been installed. We were fascinated by this new marvel and spent hours daring one another to touch it. For some reason, I had a tolerance for the electric current and gained great status among my peers by being able to grip, hold and take the current for several seconds. This "dare you" contest came to a halt when one daredevil did the ultimate and urinated on it and caused himself no little injury as a result.

Considerable time was spent damming up these ponds to make them even deeper, and the owners of the property spent considerable time undamming them and chasing us buck-naked swimmers away. One very sadistic person, who shall remain nameless, filled the hole on his property with barbed wire. This certainly was not conducive to swimming and achieved its purpose of keeping us boys out of the stream and adjacent cornfield until a summer flood came along and washed it out.

When the spring rains brought high water, the gentle creek became a swift and savage river which overran the banks and washed away crops and sometimes bridges. I remember once trying to cross it with some friends in a large wagon when the current was swollen and the wagon was carried away like a plaything. We found its shattered remains three miles downstream. And it was a miracle we weren't drowned in the mishap.

The creek provided other activity. Large fish traps were set in the summer and steel traps in the winter. Sometimes muskrats were caught and, once in a great while, a mink. Muskrat hides sold for 50 cents each, but a good mink pelt brought $10.00.

My Uncle Hoyle trapped to supplement the Bryson income and was recognized as one of the better trappers. Taylor Ledford, a colorful mountaineer, was another outstanding trapper, as was Homer Bryson. They caught everything from bobcats to skunks and sold the hides to Jake Plott in Blairsville. Jake also would buy ginseng and, because he knew all these mountain men, he was a man of political influence.

Most of the trapping I did was with "rabbit boxes," which were wooden contraptions like big shoeboxes with drop doors on one end which were sprung shut with stick triggers. I would bait them with carrots or apples and set them in rabbit paths in the pastures and pine forests. The best places were where rabbits crossed under rail fences—spots you could find easily because the rabbits would bite off some of the wood as they went under.

Many frosty mornings I got up early to check my rabbit boxes before going to school, and I was diligent because, if I caught one, I could sell it for a dime at the store. Needless to say, however. I didn't get rich because the rabbits were too smart to get caught unless they were very young or very hungry.

A more reckless form of recreation was "riding pines." This consisted of finding dense pine thickets—of which there were many in and around Young Harris—and climbing up a pine tree until it bent far enough for you to swing onto another tree. This was repeated time and again until the rider either traversed the width of the thicket—which was seldom—or fell upon his you-know-what—which was often.

This always was on someone else's property, and the reactions of the owners when they caught us "riding" their pines were predictable as were those of the parents when subsequently advised of their sons' trespasses and transgressions. Many a lad, myself included, consequently found himself getting an additional overlay of red on a posterior that already was black-and-blue.

Haylofts were a favorite gathering place for the boys where the taboo against smoking was violated. The best smoke came from rabbit tobacco, which was the favorite ingredient of our "cigarettes" that we rolled with newspapers or pages from the Sears-Roebuck catalog (for which other uses will be mentioned subsequently), but corn tassels and grapevines were acceptable substitutes.

A boy was really "growed up" if he carried a can of Prince Albert smoking tobacco in his back pocket; and, if he was skillful at "rolling your own," he was truly the envy of his peers.

Some permitted their children to build "flying jennies." These were made of boards with holes drilled in the centers and then placed on poles or tree stumps with metal stobs as pivots. One person would sit on each end, and someone would push them around and around—like a merry-go-round except much faster. "Jennies" were extremely dangerous and sometimes riders would get "slung" off or the whole contraption would fly off the axis. It is a miracle there were no more broken bones than there were.

Another game called "Fox and Hound" sometimes would go from early morning until after dark. It was one in which one or more participants would take a Sears-Roebuck catalog and, with a 30-minute head start, would leave a trail of pieces of paper for another individual or group to track.

Sears-Roebuck catalogs had a more practical use, however. Inasmuch as few families could afford toilet tissue, the old catalog was taken to the outhouse for utility purposes as soon as each new one came in.

At my house we used an outdoor toilet until I was in college. There was no indoor plumbing and baths were taken in galvanized washtubs. In the summer these were filled with water and placed in a sunny spot in the yard to heat. (Solar energy is not new to the mountains!) In the winter, the water would be heated in a giant kettle. When I got older, I would go up to the Young Harris College campus and use the showers while the students were in the dining hall at mealtimes.

During the summers there, one could make some money picking blackberries and selling them for two cents a pound at a local store which resold them for making wine. It took a long time to pick a pound of blackberries because they have little weight and pack down tight. I remember one summer Jane, my sister, picked enough to buy school supplies for the fall, and I once picked enough in a week's time to buy a small can of fruit cocktail which to me is a great delicacy to this day.

The first "real" job I had was working during the summer with a timber-cutting crew. It paid $3.00 a day or $15.00 a week.

Being the youngest person working, I was assigned the job of "swamper"—the person who trimmed the tree after it was felled and cut out the underbrush so the mule drivers could get to it and "snake" it through the forest to the sawmill. This was before the days of power saws, and I was in great awe of the skilled sawyers and axmen.

My ambition at one time was to be a "lead chipper." He was the person who went ahead of the cutters and made deep gaps in each tree to be cut so it would fall in the right direction.

Swamping was back-breaking work and an indelible lesson to me in what a dollar meant and how hard each one was to come by.

A mountain sawmill was an unforgettable operation. A gasoline motor would turn the huge, threatening circular saw with its wicked, razor-sharp teeth of which I recently was reminded when I saw the movie "Jaws." The off-bearers were kept busy stacking the boards as they were sawed. It was dangerous work and human limbs were broken and even sawed off from time to time. Many a man got the nickname "Nub" as the result of losing an appendage in a sawmill mishap.

One of the highlights of summers was the tent shows which would come to town. Every night for a week for the price of a nickel you could see Bob Steele, Ken Maynard, Tim McCoy and the other exciting and much-imitated cowboy stars chase the outlaws right off the screen and always get the girl.

The nearest theater was in Murphy, North Carolina, 20 miles away, and I got to go only once or twice a year. A movie was shown on the college campus on Friday nights, and the town youngsters would attend and occupy the front row. That was before popcorn was a movie staple, and we made nuisances of ourselves. Before the movies were halfway through we would start pushing one another on the wooden benches on which we sat. The only object was to crush the spectators at the other end of the bench, and the result sometimes was our expulsion.

We also looked forward to the summer revivals. I belonged to the Methodist Church which held its services in the college chapel, and I considered Methodist revivals boring compared to the more lively Baptist services that my friends attended.

The oratory at these revivals was impressive and often soul-stirring. I can still remember the emotionalism of the invitational hymns that were sung as the deacons asked each and every person, "Are you saved?"

Hoke Byers was one of the evangelists. He had a loud-speaker on his car, and I really was impressed when he would come through town with gospel music playing and making urgent appeals for one and all to come to the service that night.

The baptizings which followed also were colorful and well-attended occasions. These usually were performed at Townsend's Mill Pond. The preacher would wade out up to his waist, and then the newly-saved sinners—mostly boys and girls and sometimes an adult—would go out in their new clothes. He would take them in his arms, pronounce their baptism in the "Name of the Father, the Son and the Holy Ghost" and immerse them deep. There would be singing and "amens" from the bank as they staggered to the bank, sputtering, dripping and struggling to maintain their dignity.

Of all the good times I had growing up in the mountains, none stands out in my memory more than the baseball games. They not only were the highlight of my youth but also continued to be an important part of my life, even while I was teaching at YHC.

Without question, the hours spent on the skinned mountain infields of North Georgia, Eastern Tennessee and Western North Carolina were some of the happiest times of my entire life.

Each community had a "town team," and six or eight of them usually would form a league. Some of the players were excellent athletes who played a good brand of baseball. There would be the combination of young and old playing together; and, at one time, I was the youngest at 14 and Tom Jenkins in his 50's was the oldest on the Young Harris team.

In Andrews, North Carolina, one of our big rivals, Dave Bristol, an outstanding professional baseball manager in Cincinnati, Milwaukee and Atlanta, was in his early teens and Jess Mashburn was nearer to 50.

Local merchants would buy the uniforms and put their names on the backs of the shirts for advertising. I could not have been prouder wearing the New York Yankees' pinstripe than I was when I got the gray wool flannel uniform with "M. C. Hood Gen. Mdse." printed on the back. The baseball cap with "YH" on it was my status symbol—one that I wore everywhere, even to church.

Games were played on Saturday and Sunday afternoons, and road trips were made in the backs of trucks. The playing fields were usually on creek bottoms or where someone had graded off the top of a mountain. They would be leveled before the game with a car or truck pulling a wooden drag with two or three kids riding on it.

The field in Young Harris had a creek behind home plate and out in left field. Balls frequently would be hit into the creek and had to be dried off before play could be resumed. Sluggers like Hoyle Bryson and Quinton Nichols sometimes would hit them over the creek. Quinton once hit one over the walnut tree in center field, a blast remembered to this day by the old-timers.

At the end of the summer, tournaments would be held and sometimes teams would bring in a "ringer," a good player from far-away Clarkesville or Westminster, South Carolina, who would be paid as much as $10.00.

Most of the town's citizens would come to each game and sit on the wooden bleachers or up on the hill underneath the pines. On game days I would put on my uniform soon after breakfast, and one player would wear his the whole weekend without taking it off.

One of the biggest games of the season for Young Harris was with the Bean Creek Negroes. It usually would be played on July 4th, and people would come from miles around. It was the only game of the season for which admission would be charged. At the others, the hat was passed and spectators could donate whatever they desired or could afford. This also was done when a player hit a home run.

Bean Creek is located in an isolated section of White County near the present Alpine Village of Helen. A small group of blacks had lived in that section for many years, many of them descended from slaves who operated a cheese factory on nearby Tray Mountain before the War Between the States.

They were a clannish group who enjoyed life and played baseball with a reckless abandon. They realized they were crowd-pleasers and often resorted to showmanship like the big third baseman, "Moon," who tipped his hat to the crowd after a prodigious home run.

This was before Jackie Robinson broke the race barrier in professional sports, and neither they nor we realized that we were doing anything unusual in mixing the races on an athletic field. We had great times and became fast friends. We were drinking from the same water dipper while there were still "white" and "colored" signs up throughout the South on water fountains and restrooms. We were feasting on barbecued chicken together, which was a ritual before the game when we visited Bean Creek, 15 years before sit-ins resulted in integration of lunch counters in the rest of the South.

So, growing up in the mountains gave me an appreciation for hard work, the environment and my fellowman. Not bad lessons for any youth.

# IV

# Birdie and the House

*The reason firm, the temperate will,*
*Endurance, foresight, strength, and skill*
*A perfect woman, nobly planned,*
*To warn, to comfort, and command.*

*She Was a Phantom of Delight*
William Wordsworth

Mountain women are strong. Mountain women are independent. Mountain women are of a tough moral fiber.

My mother, Birdie Bryan Miller, although not mountain born, has those qualities. Simply put, she's the most determined person I've ever known.

Born in 1893 on a spacious South Carolina farm, she had a pleasant childhood in a large family. Her mother died when Birdie was a child, and her father married again relatively soon. Half brothers and sisters soon added to the growing Bryan clan.

A hard-working and fairly prosperous farmer, her father was determined that his children would have the benefit of the education he lacked.

Birdie, the tomboy of the family (she had four stair-step sisters), discovered early that she had a talent for art. To her father, this third child was an enigma. She could run faster and work harder than any others yet, at the same time, had this thing about drawing pictures. He urged her to pursue it, saw that she finished college and sent her to New York City to study at the prestigious Art Students League.

To a young woman reared in a plantation-like atmosphere, the Empire City was worldly. But she found the boys attractive and learned not to blush when she sketched nude women—or even men wearing skimpy loin cloths.

Like thousands of artists before and after, Birdie Bryan soon discovered that there was no great demand for her talents. Jobs for artists were scarce everywhere and in Leesville, South Carolina, non-existent.

It was at this time that she came across the ad in an educational bulletin about an art teacher needed at a mountain college named Young Harris over in Georgia.

She responded, was accepted and found herself in the early fall of 1919 pulling into the railroad depot at Murphy, North Carolina, at 3:00 o'clock in the afternoon and an hour late from Asheville. A three-seater stagecoach, drawn by two big black mules, awaited her. The seats were filled with students, and the driver seemed a little miffed that he had had to wait.

He started the mules in a gallop. The road from Murphy to Young Harris, then as now, curves along the high bluffs above the Little Tennessee River. My mother remembers vividly thinking that the "hack," as it was called, would plunge any minute to the rocky river below. From Murphy to Young Harris by stagecoach is six hours, and it was 9 o'clock that night when the driver pulled onto the college campus.

The new art teacher was fed and given a room in the girls' dormitory. The next morning, when she looked around at her new surroundings, it was love at first sight. The flat-land South Carolina girl was in the mountains, and they would be her home for more than a half-century.

She met some other faculty members at breakfast in the dining room. Two of the new teachers were a sister and brother, Verdie and Grady Miller, who were later to be her best friend and her husband.

When registration began, eight students signed up for art. One youngster, an orphan who because of his age lived in the girls' dormitory, wanted to take art but did not have the two dollars. He was invited to take it anyway and went on to become a significant Southern artist. An original by Leroy Jackson hangs in my mother's mountain home with the inscription on the back that reads: "To my dear friend, Mrs. Grady Miller, through whose kindness and that of her late husband a beautiful world was opened up for me."

It has already been related how the friendship with the reticent Miller sister blossomed into a romance with the brother and how the young couple began married life in a college apartment on the Emory campus at Oxford. If Dr. Sharp and Grady Miller were glad to go back to YHC in 1922, Birdie was ecstatic. The happiest years of her life were beginning.

My mother and father, during the eleven years they lived together, spent less than two years in a house. They never owned a house and their home was the campus, usually in a small apartment. The longest they lived anywhere was in a three-room apartment in Hamby Hall.

This may have been one reason that the young widow was so determined to design and build a permanent dwelling for herself and her two children—one so sturdy and enduring that it would last forever. She sought to build a monument, not just a house.

When my father died suddenly in March 1932, he left his wife and two children no land, no home, no furniture and hardly any material possessions at all. An insurance policy provided $1,000 cash and $50 per month. He also left her $90 in cash, but expenses and an old debt which mother paid more than exhausted that.

Not far from where I was born is a creek that flows from the foot of Double Knob down through dense laurel thickets, pastures and the old baseball diamond. It finally joins Brasstown Creek and then flows into the Little Tennessee River and ultimately into the Gulf of Mexico.

In this creek were, and still are, thousands of the most beautiful rocks one ever has seen. Polished by the swiftly flowing, clear mountain water, the rocks come in all shades of brown, gold and amber. No one but an artist—a penniless one like my mother—would have dreamed in 1932 of using those rocks to build a house.

The creek ran through the property of a good friend, Callie Nichols. Although a little surprised when asked, she readily agreed to let the recent widow have all the rocks she wanted. So, through the summer of 1932, my mother waded in the cold mountain water selecting rock after rock and piling them on the creek bank. Mrs. Nichols held me in her lap or laid me in the sun on the creek bank and Jane played nearby while hour after hour, a determined 39-year old widow, trained as an artist at the Art Students League in New York, waded and stooped and lifted and carried.

The carefully selected stones later were pulled by a wooden sled to the nearest dirt road where on Saturday the college truck would carry them to the broomsedge field my mother had bought with a little down but mostly on credit.

The lot she had chosen was as close to the college campus as she could buy. It was rocky and filled with broomsedge. An old fence, matted with honeysuckle, surrounded it. A rough dirt road ran in front of it to Hiawassee. Another to the side went to Murphy, North Carolina, the one she had come in on as an eager young teacher 13 years earlier.

It was during the worst of the Depression. Labor was cheap and men would work for a dollar or two a day. She drew her own plans, explained to the builders that she had only about $700 and they were to build until that was used up.

The money lasted long enough to get the rocks laid, a roof on, the windows in and one room finished. Everything else was left as was: naked rafters, sub-flooring and a stairwell that was more like a ladder. There was no bath-room and no plumbing. The first night we lived in the room that was finished, a stray dog came in and ate the butter out of a dish.

The house stayed very much this way, with a few im-provements, until I was in college. Let me emphasize, how-ever, that it was a joy to live in. You didn't have to worry about soiling the carpet or scratching the floor. You could stack fodder in the corners for Halloween parties, and one time we put a chicken brooder in the living room corner and raised chickens in it.

The biggest disadvantage was the heating of it. One solitary fireplace provided the heat during the early days, and I was almost out of grammar school before we had the comfort of a wood heater. To this day, warmth is a luxury to me that no one can understand.

My mother, with her artist's creativity, did things that amazed our neighbors. She built a beautiful rock outdoor barbecue pit and a large fish pond which she indulged with the luxuries of lily pads and goldfish. She built a lattice around the outdoor toilet and planted grapevines which climbed on it. She experimented with all kinds of flowers and shrubs—cherry, fig, pear and peach trees; raspberries; hollyhocks and an unusual fir tree which was our outdoor Christmas Tree.

Her imagination conceived all kinds of beauty that made our yard different and that neighbors soon began to emulate. The practical was interwoven with the beautiful. I remember one year the whole front yard was planted with field peas.

It was only natural that she started the first Garden Club in Young Harris.

She continued to pick up rocks by the tens of thou-sands. Frank Ervin once commented about how she could bend over—that it was "different from other people." And well it should have been with all the practice she had!

I can remember wishing as a child that she were more like other mothers—mothers who were not muscular with gnarled hands, who did not work from daylight until dark, who got their house chores done and sat on the front porch.

My mother never *sat* anywhere! She was always on the go—doing something—usually at a fast trot.

My childhood was pleasant and without regimen to it. We ate when we were hungry. I had few chores because mother did everything herself and preferred it that way.

For three years during this period she supplemented her $50-a-month income by working as a clerk in the post office for another $50 a month. After that, she sold subscriptions for magazines.

Another way she made a little money was by renting out the upstairs to people for short periods of time. I did not like this because that was where the wood heater was.

Her sisters helped us some financially, and we were fortunate in that we had a number of cousins whose clothes were handed down to us. Always at Christmas we would get presents from the aunts, who thought their sister was a little crazy staying in the mountains and trying to rear two children on less than $100 a month.

My sister finished high school in 1942 and began to talk with 16-year-old enthusiasm about going to Atlanta and getting a job in a defense plant. She appealed to my mother's patriotic streak. (Mother had volunteered as a canteen girl during World War I and was awaiting her passport when the Armistice was signed.) She also appealed to my mother's desire to get out of debt. She still owed for the land and as she put it, "I wanted to be able to dig where I please."

So, in the summer of 1942, we moved to Atlanta. Both my mother and sister got jobs making buckles for gas masks with Southern Aviation on North Avenue. We lived in a tiny apartment on Spring Street, where Jane slept on a couch and I slept with my mother.

Jane went to night school at Georgia Evening College. Sundays were our days of fun and adventure. We would go to Grant and Piedmont Parks, ride on trolley cars to the ends of the lines (we didn't own a car until I was 21 years old) and attend movies. And a treat I always shall remember was once when Birdie took us to Sunday lunch at the Biltmore Hotel!

Later, Birdie went to work at the Bell Bomber Plant as an inspector. Regularly each month she and Jane sent money back to the bank to pay off the note on our land. Sometimes that did not leave enough to buy groceries through the next pay day.

At those times we had to rely on our mountain ingenuity. Once I remember selling coathangers for a penny each to a laundry down on Techwood Avenue and buying cheese and crackers with the proceeds. Another time we came up with the idea of using our charge-a-plate at Davison's and dined like millionaires on smoked salmon and other such delicacies which were the only food available at the department store.

When the war ended, Mother and I returned to Young Harris, and Jane went on to LaGrange College, where my Aunt Verdie had been teaching for years.

I shall never forget that trip back.

Uncle Fletcher came for us in his pick-up truck, and the move was reminiscent of a scene from *The Grapes of Wrath*. All our possessions were piled on the back with rope holding the chairs and cardboard boxes together. Among my belongings were a pet chicken named Winston and a green snake that had no name.

I hated to leave Atlanta and the new friends I had made, but I soon fell back into the mountain way of living. Mother was overjoyed because she had her yard to dig in and we were out of debt for the first time in our lives.

Plans that had been forming in her mind during our cooped-up life in the small city apartment began to be implemented. The most grandiose by far was enlarging the basement, which always had been too small to her thinking. She decided to dig it the entire width and length of the house.

To help her, she recruited Mrs. Verdie Shook, a spindly

little lady who never weighed over 85 pounds and whose arms at the shoulder were no bigger than at her wrist. She had been left with a large family to provide for when her husband had been killed when a log rolled over him during timber cutting in the mountains. She had worked with mother before for hand-me-downs of our hand-me-downs and foodstuff out of our always-plentiful garden.

They first tackled the job by getting under the house on their hands and knees with a mattock, a shovel and a washtub. One would dig while the other shoveled the dirt into the washtub and dragged it out from under the house. It would be dumped in some low place on the property, and the process would be repeated time and time again. After much tortuous effort, they got the hole big and deep enough to stand in it and then to get a wheelbarrow inside. I cannot remember how many weeks it took, but Birdie's dream of a basement under her house came true.

Many years later, when my mother was in her middle 70's, she got the idea that the basement should be cemented. Dearly loving to mix concrete, she proceeded to lay a slab on the basement floor. As she had many times in the past, she mixed the cement in her beloved and much-used wheelbarrow and, with her hands, dipped and stuccoed it into the red clay walls of the basement. When it dried, the imprints of her fingers and hands were all over the walls in a surrealistic pattern worthy of Salvador Dali.

This is just another reason why Birdie's house is unique and so meaningful to me. What other son in history has his mother's fingerprints cast in concrete in the walls of his family home?

Beginning early in my boyhood, Mother was selected each election, whether it was state or local, to help at the polls. I think this was done for two reasons—it was well known that she needed the money and, just as importantly, she was one of the few that both warring political factions in Towns County trusted. So this, too, became a part of my childhood—my mother's spending every election day and into the night at the "law house," as it was called.

All elections in Towns County generated almost unbelievable competition, as I will go into detail about in a later chapter. I remember waiting huddled in a corner during the "count out" and listening to my mother call "tally" when every five votes were counted for each candidate. I also remember the politeness with which these combative, whiskered, overall-wearing men—some red-eyed from a few election-day drinks of moonshine—treated my mother, the only female in their hardened group.

It was probably from this beginning that my mother later found herself a candidate. She served on the Young Harris City Council for more than 25 years. She usually was the Treasurer or Clerk, which meant that she collected the town taxes and, later, when Young Harris got city water, the water bills.

There was a certain day to pay those bills at the "law house," but most persons preferred to drop by the house to make their payments. A young lad, living alone with his mother, learned much from such an experience. One lesson was that when a taxpayer paid his taxes, he usually had some choice comments on how that hard-earned money was to be spent.

My mother was always elected without opposition; that fact was almost unheard of in Towns County. Twice, she was elected mayor, one of the few lady mayors in Georgia. She served as one of the first vice presidents of the newly formed Georgia Municipal Association. Earlier, she had been selected as the first woman ever to serve on a jury in Towns County. Many persons, especially when I had a lady as an opponent in my race for Lieutenant Governor, have asked what I thought about liberated women and especially women in politics. Frankly, I never knew anything else.

When I was in college in YHC and walking up to the dormitory to take a shower while students were at supper, my mother decided we needed running water and an indoor bathroom. Again, she borrowed money, and an addition, which to my mind detracted from the beauty of the house, was constructed. Later, she repaid this loan by going to Macon to live with Jane and her husband and to work there.

During this time I was in the Marine Corps. For the second time the house was closed and Mother worked in another defense-related job. This time it was at Warner Robins Air Force Base, and she was in her 60's.

In the late 1950's she returned to Young Harris, and in 1959, Shirley and I and our two sons returned. For a year we lived in a college-owned home as my parents had forty years earlier.

At mother's insistence, we moved into the rock house and built Birdie one next door. Again, she designed it, drew plans and supervised the construction.

It was warmer, more comfortable than the old one but will never take its place. Birdie continues to look after both homes and was mowing the grass in both yards after she was 80 years old.

Once, without her knowledge, we came home and found the 82-year-old on the roof of her house sweeping and getting leaves out of the gutters.

In the spring of 1974 when I was planning to qualify for the office of Lieutenant Governor, I called my mother to ask if I could send someone to bring her down for the big event. She replied that she was too busy to come. After thinking about it awhile, I decided to call back. After all, what could be more important than being present when your son qualified for the second highest office in the State.

After some questioning, she replied that what she was busy doing was building a billboard in her front yard entreating all who drove by on Georgia 76 to vote for Zell Miller for Lieutenant Governor.

Still an erect, proud woman, she prefers living alone where she "can do as I please." A devoted radio listener and television viewer, she keeps up with current events, and as strong-willed as ever, she makes up her own mind on political candidates and positions on issues.

For more than a quarter of a century she served as the communion steward for Sharp Memorial Methodist Church. That meant that once a month she filled the cups with grape juice and then gathered and washed them. Only within the past year did she give up this chore. She would like to walk to Bald Mountain one more time. It is about eight miles and she's walked it almost 100 times. She walked it and carried Jane when Jane was six months old. My father was furious when he came home and found out about it.

Every morning she walks to the post office and picks up trash, papers and beer cans on both sides of the highway. She then puts her collection in the white trash cans along the way, cans that she made from barrels, painted and placed along the way years ago because she wanted the town to be pretty. She is a litterbug's worst enemy, and to this day I won't throw anything out of a car window.

I'm proud of this tough, hard-working, opinionated woman. We argue often because she reared me in her mold, and it is hard for two persons as independent as we are to agree on everything.

Psychologists tell us now that 50 percent of a child's education and training take place before the age of five and 30 percent more during the next two years. During those formative years, Birdie Bryan Miller shaped my life. The lesson was "to thine own self be true." She taught me by example the importance of perseverance, hard work, initiative and family loyalty and of recognizing that there are many things more important than material goods. It was a natural response, therefore, that in 1976 when many were urging me to run for Congress she bluntly said that she thought I ought to serve my full four-year term.

On the side porch of the house, there is a hand print of my six-year-old sister, the hand print of a six-month-old who tried to pick up the cement and written into the cement with a nail by Birdie, "Built in honor of Stephen Grady Miller, for Jane and Zell."

This was why my mother built the house and why she remained in Young Harris.

A few years ago I added this plaque to the living room:

"This house was built in memory of Stephen Grady Miller, outstanding educator and Dean of YHC, who died at age 40. It is also a monument to his brave widow, Birdie Bryan Miller, who designed it, gathered the rocks from the creek, dug and cemented the basement and made a rocky field into this beautiful place."

# V

# Young Harris College (1932 to Present)

*A college education is not a quantitative body of*
*memorized knowledge salted away in a card file. It*
*is a taste for knowledge, a taste for philosophy,*
*if you will; a capacity to explore, to question, to*
*perceive relationships between fields of knowledge*
*and experience.*

A. Whitney Griswold

I entered Young Harris College in the fall of 1945—an eighth grader among returning G. I.'s from World War II and, by my own estimation, the most insignificant of the insignificant. To my own sense of insecurity and innate shyness was added the burden of being a "town student," which meant I did not live in the dormitory and was considered a "country bumpkin" by the sophisticates from Gainesville, Atlanta and Florida who did.

But I went because it was easier to go than it was to explain to my Aunt Verdie Miller why I was not going. She was a strong-willed woman who, like my mother, was determined that my sister Jane and I were going to get an education. From the time of my earliest recollection she had been pounding into my head that my father had been "somebody" and that I was going to follow in his footsteps. I never really understood as a boy how that was going to be, but I did not question it because it was an accepted fact of my fatherless upbringing that whatever Aunt Verdie said was going to be was going to be.

Aunt Verdie continued to teach at YHC after my father died in 1932 until, during World War II after Jane had finished the Young Harris Academy and we moved to Atlanta for two years, she moved to LaGrange College, where she taught and was Dean of Women for 25 years. During that time she was a combination father-figure, friend, confidante, idol and awesome taskmaster who could be as gentle as an angel and as stern as a judge. She was more than aunt and I loved her more than anyone else except my mother.

She had been the closest to my father of all his brothers and sisters, and she shared his thirst for knowledge and his natural abilities as a teacher. And, to the degree she could, she took his place in my early life—always encouraging and guiding me and sharing with me her hopes and dreams for the family in general and me in particular. I looked up to her and would rather have died than displease her.

Until I became too old to be admitted, I visited with her regularly in her room in the girls' dormitory at YHC and during those visits learned to love the books which she shared with me. Books were her life, and her gifts to me always were books. After she left for LaGrange College, she continued to send them to me along with clippings about current events about which she thought I should be informed. She even sent me her own correspondence course when I was in high school.

Being the closest relative with a car, Aunt Verdie took us to the Miller homecomings so we would know our family, to outings at Vogel Lake and even to movies she thought worthwhile in far-away Murphy, North Carolina. Some of my fondest childhood memories are of riding beside this silver-haired angel on these various trips which were glorious boyhood adventures to me.

My shyness and insecurity as a student were compounded by the fact that some of my teachers were former students or teaching colleagues of Aunt Verdie or my father. This made both Jane and me uncomfortable because, as Miller kids, we felt we had to prove something to them and ourselves. It made things doubly difficult for me because, at that time, baseball, not studies, was my consuming interest, and fellow students who entered YHC at the same time I did to this day recall me as the skinny youngster who always had a baseball glove in hand.

An evidence of my timidity at the time is the fact that there is no photograph of me in the YHC annual for either my first or second year. I was too shy to have one made.

But the necessity of living up to the Miller image forced me to take the step which changed my life and outlook and thrust me into the evolution which brought me to the path I follow today. Although I put it off until my third year in high school and acted then only because it was a prerequisite for participation in intra-society athletics, I joined the Phi Chi Debating Society. My father had been a champion Phi Chi Debater, and it would have been unthinkable for me not to have joined or to have joined any other group.

I remember vividly the dread which bordered on fear of the debating part of the society's activities. It met once every two weeks for that purpose, and every member was expected to engage in a debate during each school year. Hoping somehow to avoid that requirement, I attended spasmodically, and I did succeed in avoiding an assignment to a debate until January, 1948, when I got caught.

Someone remembered that Miller had not had a debate, and I was assigned to participate in one on inflation two weeks thence. The prospect scared me almost to death, and my insides churned with terror for the next 14 days. But Birdie was delighted and, somehow, with her help and encouragement I managed to get a short speech down on paper and memorized it carefully. I practiced it over and over before the mirror and, as often as she had time, before Birdie. I don't think I ever had been unhappier nor she happier because her Zell was doing what she most wanted him to do.

Pale, trembling and with knees shaking, I managed to get through with my part of the debate held in the old Reid Building without disgracing Birdie or embarrassing myself. And, when it was announced my side had won, all of a sudden, like the clouds parting and the sun shining through, I awoke to the exhilaration of having an audience listening to what I was saying and applauding. I must have done better than I thought at the time because, when champion debaters were chosen a few weeks later, I was elected an alternate.

One of the young men who had been elected as a Phi Chi Champion Debater had to leave school after the winter quarter and, in the spring of 1948, as the alternate, I took his place. I had only recently turned 16, was only a junior in high school and had only that one society debate a few months earlier as speaking experience.

But I was fortunate to have two very mature and experienced colleagues—Clyde Lee, Jr., who had been on the winning debate team of the year before, and John "Luke" Dorris, who was a seasoned speaker. Their help was invaluable, and even more helpful was the assistance of Miss Edna Herren, an English and speech teacher who was the adviser to the Phi Chi and Phi Delta Societies. With the exception of my mother, my wife and Aunt Verdie, no individual has had so profound an effect on my life.

Edna Herren was a rare and gifted teacher who could make Beowulf live and who, with her instruction and encouragement, opened doors on vistas about which this mountain lad never had dreamed. Unmarried and dark-haired, she was a beauty who dressed impeccably, always wore a flower in her hair and used an intoxicating perfume which I later learned was "White Shoulders." There was an electricity about her and she was my first teen-age "crush."

I not only was fascinated by and in awe of such a

creature but also literally worshipped her and did whatever I thought would please her. She was the adviser to the school paper; so I joined its staff. She later became adviser to the yearbook; so I joined its staff. She was a fan of athletics; so I tried all the harder to be a winner on the ball field.

She believed that preparation and hard work won debates and had little patience with glib orators who relied on their gift of gab rather than doing their homework. She demanded perfection and, although I could not give her that, for the first time in my life I had a real desire to improve myself intellectually.

The debate teams were composed of three debaters each. Each speaker was limited to 15 minutes, and the last speaker on each side gave the rebuttal during his allotted time. Luke Dorris led off for the Phi Chis. I was the second speaker and the experienced Clyde Lee was third.

The debate subject was "Resolved: That Federal Aid to Education Would Not Be a Detriment to the U. S." The Young Harris Debating Society had chosen the subject, and we had elected to present the affirmative. In 1948 this was the liberal side, and I was to find myself on it in other questions during the next four years. This was to cause Chief Justice Henry Duckworth of the Georgia Supreme Court, himself a graduate of YHC and native Choestoe friend of my father's, to draw me aside one Saturday morning after a debate and say, "I hope you're not believing all this stuff you're saying."

I shall never forget the debate in 1948. I had worked myself into an emotional frenzy. The Pruitt-Barrett Building was under construction; and, late that afternoon, when I went up to take a shower in the dormitory, for some reason, I found myself climbing the scaffold to the top of the unfinished building. There, as the sun was setting over the Three Sisters Mountain, I prayed—prayed as hard as I could, not that we would win, but that I would not mess up or forget my carefully prepared and memorized speech.

Even in 1948 champion debates were still auspicious occasions, and the Susan B. Harris Chapel was packed to capacity. People stood on the porch, sat in the windows and milled around outside. It was the biggest event of the year not only at YHC but also in the community. My mother was very proud but found it hard to believe that her son, who previously had been interested only in baseball, actually was a champion debater for the Phi Chis. In her eyes, except for being a teacher, this was the greatest height anyone could achieve.

Champion debaters wore rented tuxedos; and each, after delivering his speech, went to the front of the stage where his date, sitting in the front row, would come forward and pin a carnation on his lapel.

At this time in my life, I had never dated and was truly scared of girls. However, with a lot of encouragement from my two colleagues and Miss Herren, I asked the YHC beauty queen to be my date. I could not believe she would accept and had had someone else inquire to make certain she would before I asked her.

It was a great moment, but I did not get up the courage to have another until the next champion debate a year later.

I enjoyed the high drama that went with being a champion debater. It was almost as thrilling as getting a base hit in a ball game, and I decided to work at this speech-making business a little harder.

In 1949, although only a senior in the high school, I was the veteran debater and had the responsibility of giving the rebuttal and providing leadership. That year my two colleagues were Jack Brinkley, a serious young man from South Georgia who also was a very good athlete, and Guy Sharpe, a dark-haired Mr. Personality who gained instant popularity upon his arrival at YHC. We worked well together. I was somewhere between the intense Brinkley and the personable Sharpe.

The debate concerned government regulation of broadcasting facilities. Again the Phi Chis took the liberal side and again we won. Jack spoke first and Guy was second. I concluded and gave the rebuttal for which I had prepared myself by trying to anticipate every major point that the opposition could make and writing and memorizing my responses. I probably had an hour of material memorized and used less than ten minutes of it.

That summer, after graduating from high school and winning my second champion debate, I began to have other than debating dates. I had been elected President of the Phi Chis for fall quarter and, as such, felt responsible for trying to attract some of the incoming freshmen. Two of the freshmen I wrote were outstanding basketball players recruited by Coach Luke Rushton. Bob Short made All-State in the nearby town of Clayton, and James Hutto had been an outstanding all-round athlete at Fort Valley. Both not only became Phi Chis but also extremely close friends. Short later was Prep Sports Editor of *The Atlanta Journal,* a speech writer for Carl Sanders and Lester Maddox, and manager of the first Jimmy Carter campaign in 1966.

These two excellent athletes, who also became All-State junior college basketball players, were the nucleus for some of the first great basketball teams that Coach Luke Rushton was to produce.

Rushton had graduated from YHC in 1942 and was an excellent baseball and tennis player. He came back after graduating from Presbyterian College and serving in the Navy to teach history and coach.

Young Harris was a basketball college and had produced some outstanding teams in the 1930's and early 1940's.

My Uncle Hoyle Bryson played there, participating in college games when he was still in high school. He was, without a doubt, one of the finest athletes I've ever seen, and that is not just family or community pride. Recently, I talked with Charlie Roberts who covered sports for more than 40 years for *The Atlanta Constitution* and told him that I grew up in Young Harris. Without knowing of my kinship to Hoyle, he remarked, "You know, one of the greatest athletes I ever saw came from there. His name was Hoyle Bryson." And that was from a man who had seen them all!

The team played in an old gym which, in its day, was quite an improvement over the outdoor court behind the Susan B. Harris Chapel. But in the late 1940's and early '50's, it was like a barn with two big pot-bellied stoves at each end. There were no dressing rooms, and games literally were rained out because of a leaky roof.

I had spent hours in the old gym as a youngster, crawling up through a hole in the floor when it was locked. In 1950 I made the team but logged very little playing time.

Rushton completely revitalized the athletic program. He had many contenders and won several State championships.

The year 1950 was a year of great activity. I was the President of the Phi Chis and of the Spat Club, editor of the school paper and associate editor of the yearbook. I was a "Big Man on Campus," but a little one in the classroom. My grades were poor and I know I tried the patience of such excellent teachers as Mrs. Wilma Myers and Miss Hilda McCurdy. Ralph Coker and Sanford Spier were my partners on the champion debate team which the Phi Chis again won, taking the "liberal side" of providing health care in the U.S.

In 1951 I again debated with Edgar Jenkins and Mac Haynie. We won with the unpopular negative side of whether the U.S. should reject the welfare state.

That final year, an unusual thing occurred during the last week of commencement. The Clay Medal Speaking Contest had been changed to the Miller Memorial in honor of my father, and Mother had been asked to present the trophy to the winner. For many years the competition had been held on the night preceding the Friday night champion debate. On Wednesday the Phi Chi speaker departed the campus without notice and left the Phi Chis without a speaker.

No one felt qualified to fill in on such short notice, and yet the Phi Chis did not want to give the championship to the opposing debating society by default. I volunteered to do it provided no announcement was made about the change. I quickly revived an old speech that I had used a few years before. And I won, receiving the first Miller Memorial Speech Trophy from my mother. The following night, Ed, Mac and I won the champion debate.

The next day I graduated from YHC. It was a sad day and I cried unashamedly. I had entered YHC a naive, scared country boy. With the help of Miss Herren and others, I had held practically every office on the campus, had been a winning champion debater four times and, at one time or another, had served as captain of the Phi Chi football, baseball, softball and basketball teams.

On the YHC campus I walked with a sense of pride. Perhaps cocky would be a better description; but, whatever, as long as I was in the shadow of YHC, I was confident.

However, once away from that comfortable campus, I reverted back to the shy, insecure, reticent mountain youth I really was.

I had begun my days at YHC when Professor Worth Sharp was President, and I felt a bond with this older man. Although a superb athlete, able scholar and gifted teacher, he had to live, just as I had, with being the son of a YHC giant. He had become President in 1943 and had served during the war years. In 1947 he accepted the position of Dean of Brenau College in Gainesville, where he was to remain for 30 years.

Walter Downs, a gentle, mild-mannered professional educator, was selected to replace him. He did an admirable job under difficult circumstances. He was a classroom teacher, however, and as administrator, found the fund-raising chores difficult and unpleasant.

The truth was YHC supporters were still looking for another Dr. Joe Sharp.

In 1950 they found him in Charles Clegg, who had finished YHC in the class of 1927 and in 1950 was serving as the resident in charge of the North Georgia Technical and Vocational School in Clarkesville. He was persuaded to leave that safe position to assume the presidency of a junior college that was on the ropes financially and every other way.

It was a formidable undertaking, but Charles Clegg was a formidable man. He possessed the same attributes as Dr. Sharp: he was a good speaker, able fund-raiser and effective administrator. Like Dr. Sharp, he was loved by the students and became an intimate with the townspeople. He regularly visited the loafers' bench and contributed some of the best stories. His sense of humor was beyond description. He would have made an excellent politician. He was a great college president.

Under his leadership the college grew and prospered at a rate unparalleled since the days of Dr. Sharp. He had intense interest in athletics and realized what it can add to the stature of an institution. He, therefore, gave complete support to Rushton and the athletic program. He also regenerated the interest of Scott Appleby, who again contributed to the College as he had earlier.

Religious activity always has been important to YHC, and probably no person has contributed any more to it in recent times than Dr. Dow Kirkpatrick. A scholarly, articulate man, he was brought to YHC in an effort to rebuild its religious program.

He did and more. Sharp Memorial Methodist Church and a new parsonage were constructed. An unforgettable sight was this dignified, intellectual working behind a mule with a scoop on parsonage hill.

I received a partial scholarship in political science to Emory University and in September 1951 moved into a small dormitory room on campus.

This was the most frustrating time of my life. I had

done almost too good at YHC and, on the Emory campus and later at the University of Georgia, I felt overwhelmed by the sophistication of the students. But, most of all, I was homesick for the mountains.

From the first time the family left and went to Atlanta, I could not stand to be away from the mountains. I had gotten slowly over it in Atlanta; but now, as a 20-year-old, it bothered me tremendously.

My only contact with Young Harris was the Trailways bus that traveled only on weekends. I also received letters of encouragement from Aunt Verdie and Miss Herren, the latter sending me a season ticket to the Atlanta Symphony.

I was lonely, depressed and miserable. A feeling of inferiority permeated my whole being. I well remember being in class with Rhodes Scholar Elliott Levitas and marveling at his storehouse of knowledge. After two quarters of B's and C's, I quit and returned to the solace of the mountains. I felt like a failure and could hardly face Miss Herren and others who had been so sure that I would succeed.

For the first time in my life I experimented with alcohol. It did not help. Finally, in desperation, I enlisted in the Marine Corps, determined to lick this weakness. The sign had read, "We make men," and I determined I would get into something that would either cure or kill me.

It almost killed me. To go from a background of no male figure in one's life to one dominated 24 hours a day for 12 weeks by a drill instructor at Parris Island, South Carolina, was a dramatic change.

I finished "boot camp" in November 1953 and was transferred to Camp LeJeune, North Carolina. In January, while I was home on the weekend, Shirley and I were married. Shirley Carver, of nearby Andrews, North Carolina, had come to Young Harris College as a 16-year-old high school senior in the summer of 1952 to get the remaining credits she needed for an early graduation. We had dated some that summer, and we had written to each other while I was at Parris Island. After marriage, she continued in school until graduation in June 1954. Then she joined me at Camp LeJeune, where I became a "brown bagger," the term for married Marines. Our first home was an 8' x 19' trailer in Camp Geiger Trailer Park. With the Marines and marriage, the maturing process had proceeded rapidly.

I performed various duties in the Corps. To begin with, I was in the Tenth Marines, an artillery regiment. One day I was called in by the commanding officer who, being a good public relations man like most Marines, had decided to publish a regimental newspaper and saw from my file that I had attended college. I became the editor of "The Cannoneer."

A very good friend, Eric England, from Choestoe was one of the premier marksmen on the Marine Corps rifle team. We rode back and forth home every other weekend, and he got me very much interested in shooting. With his encouragement I earned the expert rifleman's medal, something that fewer than one out of 100 Marines achieve and became a rifle instructor for a period of time. Shooting on the rifle range starts at daybreak and one is through by noon. Many days I worked on the rifle range in the morning and wrote poems under a tree in the afternoon, never really aware of the contrast of the two.

In July 1955 our first son, Murphy, was born. Shirley was with her family in Andrews because I had been sent to Great Lakes for a while and had just returned to LeJeune. I hurried home with a week's leave. As soon as possible I moved them both to be with me.

My three years' enlistment in the Marines ended in August 1956. I had moved Shirley, who was pregnant with our second child, Matthew, to Athens a few weeks earlier. I had planned to get my bachelor's degree and then go to law school.

The first quarter back in college I took Georgia History under the well-known Dr. E. Merton Coulter. Not since Miss Herren had a teacher so affected me. For the first time I understood why my father had been fascinated by history. And I decided I would become a teacher.

For three years in Athens, Shirley looked after two infants and I spent hours in the classroom and library. I also had to supplement the income we were getting from the G. I. bill.

I worked at Allen's on Prince Street as a waiter and hamburger cook from five o'clock in the afternoon until midnight for seven dollars a night. I also tutored football players.

I took every course Dr. Coulter taught, and we became great friends. While working on my Master's and later my Ph. D., I taught as an assistant in the History Department. Dr. Albert Saye, of the Political Science Department, was another close friend and teacher of influence on my life.

I cannot remember when I decided to return to YHC as a teacher. It was something that both Shirley and I took for granted that we would do some time.

With the responsibility of two sons and an opening for a history and political science teacher, I returned to YHC in the fall of 1959. As my parents did 37 years before, we lived in a house owned by the college and located across from the post office. It has now been torn down.

It was our first real home and we were thrilled with its spaciousness and large yard. My salary was $400.00 a month. I was also the adviser to the *Enotah Echoes,* the college newspaper, and later, for three years, coached the college baseball team.

It was good to be back in the mountains and especially back on the YHC campus. I was doing exactly what I wanted to do. Although I had taught at the University of Georgia, I was a little apprehensive about teaching in the same building where my father had taught and teaching with many colleagues who had been my teachers years before.

But working for Dr. Charles Clegg was a joy and a pleasure. He was an unusually tolerant man and made me feel at home and at ease. In fact, he became very much like a father.

During the 13 years of Dr. Clegg's administration, YHC flourished. His wife, Fay, whom he had met at YHC, was an able helpmate and, after his death, she continued as Alumni Secretary.

Not only Dr. Clegg and I but other boys met the girls they later married at YHC. This common practice once prompted Dr. Clegg to remark that YHC is "like a shoe factory; they come out of here in pairs."

Dr. Clegg understood the value of a loyal alumnus. His loyalty to YHC had been the only reason he had left a safe and prestigious job to come back to YHC. This loyalty, the same kind that had brought Dr. Sharp back, is what many alumni feel has made YHC unique.

Manget and Winship Halls were dormitories built in the late 1950's for the men students. In 1958, the Academy Division was dropped. In 1961, the Appleby Center for Women was completed. A modern dormitory, it replaced what originally had been called the Enotah Inn when it was built in 1912, a huge wooden structure with outside walls of tin. The name had been changed in 1928 to Appleby Hall when Mr. Scott Appleby had brick-veneered the building. Long porches ran the entire length of the building on each of the three floors, and sometimes in warm weather students slept outside.

From 1961 through 1963 I taught four courses a quarter during the fall and spring. I also taught in summer school. During winter quarter I served in the Georgia Senate. Dr. Clegg had granted me this privilege in 1960 when I had gone to him with the idea of running for the Senate.

There is no single thing that gives me greater pleasure than to spend an hour with 15 or 20 young persons in a classroom. The imparting of knowledge, the spark that sometimes is generated, the evidence of thirst for further information which sometimes is generated are a great "turn-on" for me. There is no doubt in my mind that someday I shall return to this enjoyable occupation of my parents, my grandparents and my great-grandparent.

The young persons not only were my students; they also were my friends. To this day some of the people to whom I feel closest are former students. Two extremely bright ones, Marti Plemmons Pingree and Hank Huckaby, were my sole campaign staff when I ran for Congress in 1964 and remain with me today as my Press Secretary and Senate Research Director, respectively. Many of my county campaign chairmen were former students at YHC, now successful in business and with families of their own. Nan Jared is the wife of Jimmy Carter's Press Secretary, Jody Powell; and Ronnie Milsap, a blind student from the nearby mountains of North Carolina, is one of the most famous country music artists.

In 1964 when I decided to run for the U. S. Congress, I resigned from the position I then had as Alumni Affairs Director and chief recruiter of students. I had enjoyed getting to travel to various high schools but missed the classroom a great deal.

In 1967 Charles Clegg died of a heart attack. Dr. Raymond Cook became President, and he was followed by Dr. Douglas Sasser. Both were former YHC students and able men but, as it had been when Dr. Sharp had died, there were giant shoes to fill and it was inevitable that all successors for a while would be compared with Dr. Clegg.

Buildings were renovated and the new Charles R. Clegg Fine Arts Auditorium was built in 1965 as a fitting memorial to this great man who first began raising the money for this $600,000 structure.

Because of the number of junior colleges built in the 1960's in Georgia, it became more difficult to attract students from places like Gainesville, which by then had its own junior college.

As a State Senator I had been the author of a resolution which set up a committee to study the feasibility of the State contributing a certain amount to students attending the various private colleges throughout the State. It was obvious that any student educated by private colleges saved that much for the State. Our committee's recommendation was that the State fund private tuition grants to such students. In 1969 this became law and helped save not only YHC but many other private colleges in Georgia as well.

Dr. Ray Farley became President of YHC in 1971. He had served on the faculty for a number of years. By all criteria, he has done an excellent job. The enrollment of 540 students is capacity. They come from more than 100 counties in Georgia and several other states. Today's campus of approximately 185 naturally beautiful acres, dotted by more than 20 modern structures, is valued at more than $3 million. A new $1,500,000 building is being planned for math, business administration and science. It will be named The Maxwell Center for Alva and Edna Maxwell, longtime benefactors of YHC.

More importantly, the tradition begun by Reverend Artemus Lester and Judge Harris and nurtured by the likes of Dr. Joe Sharp and Dr. Charles Clegg continues. More than bricks and mortar, it is a college where the individual still counts, an institution which strives to educate the total person.

# VI

# Mountain Dialect

*Your Mountains build their monuments*
*Though ye destroy their dust.*

*The Bell of the Atlantic*
Lydia Huntley Sigourney

As a barefoot boy growing up in the mountains of Young Harris before the time of television and without a male companion at home, I spent many, many hours hanging around what is known as the "loafers' bench" at the country store where every night a dozen or more men would gather after the day's work in the fields or woods to gossip, talk politics, tell tall tales and generally "chaw the fat."

In the summer it was outside on a bench and on nail kegs; in the winter, inside around a pot-bellied stove. The locale changed from time to time—first at Leon's, then at Homer Howell's and then at John Cochran's—but Leon's "bench" was the most imposing. It was at least 10 feet long and from one end to the other the edges were carved by the whittlers' knives into impressive designs which changed from day to day according to the moods and talents of the occupants at any given time. It was an adventure in itself just going down to see what the day's idle sculpturing had wrought.

The faces of the "loafers" changed according to the time of the day, week, month and year as well as the vicissitudes of mountain life; but the conversations, even when the stories were outrageous lies, were always fascinating. I didn't mind a bit being the only boy there or being called "the young-un" and teased about not having "enuf whiskers to be licked off by a kittycat."

Some of the regulars would come early on the days they had good stories to tell, and they would tell them over and over, embellishing them with each telling, as each shift of listeners came in. Often the final versions were so much better than the first ones that the originators would go away convinced in their own minds that that was the way the events really occurred. Listening to these yarns develop was not unlike having a kaleidoscope in which the dramatic pictures were made by words instead of colors.

There were so many good ones that I would not hazard a choice as to the best and most colorful storyteller in Choestoe and environs. But the champion listener without contest was Mr. Jack Benfield.

Upon arrival and before settling down to his reserved place on the "bench" which no knowing participant would usurp, Mr. Jack would buy himself an "RC Dope" and a "hunk o' rat cheese" from the hoop of cheddar cheese which was a staple in every country store and always occupied a prominent place on a round cutting board with a cleaver-like knife on the main counter.

He would then sit down, nod to his companions and proceed to eat the cheese slowly and deliberately, alternating with swallows from his drink and every so often lifting the bottle above his head to peer contemplatively through the bottom at its remaining contents. All the while he was listening intently but never uttered a sound except for the loud belch he emitted upon completion of his snack.

When there was a lull in the yarn-spinning, he would look around as if to ask if that were all and, unless someone launched into an interesting topic, he would nod to his companions, get up and leave the same way he came—without a word.

My mother was horrified by the whole business. She was afraid I would learn cuss words and I did—a whole vocabulary of them, some so quaint and provincial that when I used them after leaving the mountains nobody knew what I was talking about.

But I learned much more because the language I heard and spoke on those occasions was the colorfully expressive and beautifully archaic dialect of the Southern mountains. At that time, however, I was wholly oblivious to either its unique simplicity or its historic genesis, and it was not until I became a graduate student that I became aware that it was a tongue apart with roots in the classic tradition of Chaucer and Shakespeare, and then I appreciated the significance.

But in growing up, I thought everybody talked that way.

My first awakening to the fact that such was not the case came when my mother moved us to Atlanta during World War II and I attended a city elementary school where, on the first day, I was laughed at for calling the brown paper bag in which I carried my lunch a "poke" and for saying I was "toting" rather than carrying it.

Later, in the Marine Corps as a young man, I got a look from my commanding officer, a graduate of Boston College, that I remember to this day when I referred to being in a hurry as "being in a swivet."

My first reaction to the smiles, wisecracks and mocking which greeted my mountain idiom was shame, but it gradually gave way to pride as I grew up to realize it was not a corruption of modern speech but part of a pioneer language which represented a colloquial survival and evolution of Elizabethan English. And, while my own usage, in public at least, long since has been tempered by contemporary construction and modern jargon, I still treasure the heritage of it, often lapse into it and no longer make a conscious effort to hide it.

Since being in the public eye, I have no single personal characteristic that has been more noticed than the way I talk and some of the mountain phrasing which naturally creeps into my speech.

Former *Atlanta Constitution* Editor Reg Murphy described it as the "flavor of the Blue Ridge in his voice," and his successor, Hal Gulliver, has referred to me as "Zell Miller of the North Georgia twang." And longtime WSB Newsman Aubrey Morris has not been even that kind; he says that the three worst voices in Georgia are his, former Mayor Ivan Allen, Jr.'s and mine.

It no longer bothers me to be kidded about my mountain expressions. In fact, I have come to regard them as status symbols because who else do we have running around in public life today who speaks the language of Chaucer and Shakespeare as distilled, literally and figuratively, by two centuries of Georgia Mountain usage?

But I am saddened to realize that mountain speech like the epoch which produced it is fast going the way of the languages of other ancient civilizations bypassed by time and change. Shakespeare, who, if not the father, certainly was the midwife of it, would have recognized these forces in the words from *A Midsummer Night's Dream* as "the true beginning of our end."

Its death knell was first sounded by the invasion of communication by radio, was heightened by the trespass of highways which brought the automobile and of hydroelectric dams which impounded the waters that lured the tourists and summer residents, and was climaxed by the leveling saturation of the electronic marvel and intellectual monster that is television.

All mankind is the loser in that little in the way of written history survives these admirable, hearty and hardy original Americans who are without annals except for their ballads and folktales which have been handed down by word of mouth. There are no archives to which students today can go to trace their genealogy or to recreate the details of their struggles against harsh nature, and there is no prospect of future archaeologists uncovering some counterpart of the Dead Sea Scrolls to reveal the secrets of the generations of isolation. The few remaining survivors of this culture are now so aged and so isolated in remote mountain coves that there is little likelihood that any scholar will be able to put together a chronicle of the mountain people by interviewing them.

That is why I have undertaken to put down on paper what I know and have been told about these men and women of the Southern Mountains and particularly about their dialect and provincialisms of speech. It would be a betrayal of a heritage I revere if I left it for future historians to judge this great segment of American culture by cruel and shallow parodies like the comic strip "Snuffy Smith" or by overdrawn stereotypes patterned for ridicule and low humor like the television program "Beverly Hillbillies." Even the great contemporary poet and author James Dickey has contributed to this false image of mountain people by portraying them as depraved and amoral cretins in his popular book *Deliverance.*

The mountain people are descendants of the Scotch-Irish who were driven out of Northern Ireland by the Stuart Kings. They landed in Maryland and Virginia and migrated westward as far as the hostile Indians and French would allow and then moved southward into the heart of the region of rugged mountains and beautiful valleys we now know as Appalachia. They were accompanied and followed by Virginia English, Huguenots, Pennsylvania Quakers, Polatine Germans and various dissatisfied Protestant sects.

They were the first Americans to fall back on their own resources and, as they settled in isolation from the remainder of the nation and the world and from all but their closest neighbors among themselves, their language, customs, character, possessions, knowledge and tools were isolated with them and suspended in time and thus insulated from the evolution which commerce, communication and intercourse with others normally brings. In short, they became an unchanging microcosm of eighteenth-century thought, culture and mores. For more than 200 years the only changes they knew were those of birth and death.

The mountaineers possessed the Anglo-Saxon and Anglo-Celtic qualities which formed the fundamental elements of pioneer American character—love of liberty, personal courage, capacity to withstand and overcome hardship, unstinted hospitality, intense family loyalty, innate humor and trust in God. If it could be said that they had one overriding characteristic, it would have to be independence; and they developed as extreme, rugged individualists who never closed their doors, had inherent self-respect, were honest and shrewd, knew no grades of society and had unconscious and unspoiled dignity which was utterly without pretension or hypocrisy.

Above all, they loved their beautiful mountains as they loved the members of their families. And in their archaic tongue they would say of their homes and of themselves:

"Hit's rough and raggedy, but hit's sweet home to us-uns."

"We'uns pore folk and haint got much, but you-uns welcome to what they is."

If Shakespeare could have been reincarnated in nine-teenth-century Choestoe, he would have felt right at home. The open fireplaces, spinning wheels, handmade looms, Greek lamps and good, if sometimes ungrammati-cal, Elizabethan English would all have been quite familiar to the Bard of Avon and, with the exception of having to adapt to homespun clothes, he would have had little diffi-culty assimilating into mountain society.

In fact, I have no doubt, he would have hit it off in the twentieth century with my Uncle B. H. Miller, who was a barber in Blairsville for many years and who enthralled me with his colorful stories as he gave me free haircuts. His lively language was straight out of the Choestoe of 100 years earlier and, in the words of Shakespeare in *Much Ado About Nothing,* "He was wont to speak plain and to the purpose."

If he had known him, Shakespeare probably would have made him a character in one of his plays.

I remember his saying that some man "wuz sich a liar, he'd hafta git sommon else to holler in his hawgs," and, once in a discussion about a particularly controversial trial during court week, he allowed as how "I ain't no judge and taint enuf o' me to be no jury." He was always putting me on about having a "doney gal," an Old English term for sweetheart which had its origin with British sailors who spent time in Spanish ports courting the senoritas or "donnas" as they called them.

His conversation was sprinkled with mountain words like *nary, yonder* and *fetch,* which come from Shakespeare, and *pert, atwix* and *smidgen,* which were right out of *The Canterbury Tales.*

Another character who would have intrigued Shakespeare would have been "Hub" Bryson, the tough brother of my Uncle Hoyle. "Hub" had a quick temper and when he was angry with a person, he would say, "He makes the trigger of my rifle itch." He was every inch a man, never wore a coat even in the coldest of winter and was killed while working as a linesman for the REA.

Mountain speech is primarily a spoken rather than a written language and needs to be heard to be fully appreciated. It is excessively clipped and requires extensive use of the apostrophe to indicate dropped final consonants and the merging of two or more words into one; for example, "I'm a'comin' d'reck'ly." Thus, written down, it sometimes comes out looking like gibberish while, to the ear, it makes perfect sense.

Mrs. Wilma Myers, a mountain native who was an English teacher many years at YHC, pointed out that students of it have identified some 800 dialectal or obsolete words which had their origin in Elizabethan phraseology—many of them used in almost exactly the same sense as by Shakespeare, Spenser and Marlowe. Some of them go back as far as Chaucer and Layamon.

Analysis of these words and phrases and of the

contexts in which they were used in the mountains shows there are certain consistent characteristics which indicate more form in their construction than would appear from merely listening to them being spoken.

Principal among these is the preponderant use of the Old English strong and preterit (archaic) past tenses—using *begun* instead of *began*, *drunk* instead of *drank*, *swum* instead of *swam* in the first instance and now-extinct words like "holp" for *helped*, "shuk" for *shook*, "friz" for *froze*, "fit" for *fought* in the second.

The mountain preacher who prayed: "Holp us as Thou holped our fathers" had a classic precedent in Shakespeare's "We were holp hither" from *The Tempest*. And the mountain boy who declared, "I clum up that aire ridge," could point to Chaucer as proof of the correctness of his usage.

Another common characteristic is the use of regular construction of irregular verbs in the past tense. This would be evident in the use of "throwed" instead of *threw*, "knowed" instead of *knew*, "growed" instead of *grew*, "choosed" instead of *chose* and the like. This has its corollary in application of regular construction to verbs that do not change in tense, notably *born*. It is very common to hear a mountaineer say, "I was borned in April."

Some other major characteristics and examples of them include the following:

Double past tense of regular verbs or adding an extra "ed" to past tense verbs—"drowneded" instead of *drowned*, "tosseded" instead of *tossed*, "yelleded" instead of *yelled*, etc. This is due largely to the mountain tendency to substitute a "t" or a "d" for the final consonant in a present tense verb ending in double "s" or double "l." Thus in the mountain vernacular *toss* would become "tost" and then be put into the past tense as a regular verb resulting in "tosted;" or yell would become "yeld" and then "yelded."

Use of "done" instead of *have* in the past perfect

tense—"I done done it" would be used instead of "I have done it." "I done wrote it" instead of "I have written it" and "I done said it" instead of "I have said it" are standard mountain constructions.

Use of double nouns—the terms biscuit-bread, ham-meat, tooth-dentist, women-folks, preacher-man, church-house, rifle-gun, hose-pipe, etc., are universally preferred to the single noun in the Highlands. My mother has always been referred to as a widow-woman since my father's death.

Use of double and multiple negatives—"That boy ain't never knowed nothin' about nothin' nohow;" "I ain't never seed no men-folks do no kind of washin' nowhere;" and "I ain't never gon do nothin' like that nohow, noway, noplace, notime" are very common in the mountain idiom.

Double-barrelled pronouns—perhaps the most universally recognized mountain usage is the adding of suffixes of "uns" and "all" to pronouns; hence, we-uns, us-uns, you-uns, we-all, you-all, them-all. A variation of this form is adding the suffix "un" to adjectives describing people and used as nouns, like "young-un" or "He's a tough-un." In this sense the "un" or "uns" is a corruption of "one" or "ones."

The you-all has its counterpart in the "yawl" more commonly associated with the cotton-growing areas of the flatlands.

Use of nouns and adjectives as verbs—those are as unusual as the imaginations of the speakers. "That deer'll meat me a month" and "The moon fulls tonight" are good examples.

Plurals of nouns and verbs with "es" and "ies" instead of "s"—this is the most classic reversion to Chaucerian English and is exemplified by beasties, postes, nesties, twistes, costes and in plurals of similar words ending in "t."

Use of final "n" instead of "s" on possessive pronouns—another well-known mountain construction is the use of his'n, her'n, our'n, your'n, etc., instead of his, hers, ours and yours. The origin of this form is as obscure as its usage is prevalent.

Use of verbs as adjectives—"She's the talkines' woman" and "He's the workines' man" illustrate the point.

Dropping of final "g" and "t" on participles and super-latives—*best* thus becomes "bes';" *most,* "mos';" *calling,* "callin';" *falling,* "fallin';" and, almost without exception, the entire vocabulary of such words is spoken with this slurring of the ending consonant.

Use of common words in a peculiar sense—falling in this context would be such usages as "call" for *name,* "stove" for *jabbed,* "ashamed" for *bashful,* "aim" for *intend,* "spell" for *time* or *while,* "reckon" for *think* and "fix" for *prepare, repair* or a *condition.* Most of these are from Shakespeare and Chaucer and some can be traced to Spenser, Milton, Bacon and Burns. Shakespeare, for example, had Othello saying, "I aim to," which is one of the commonest mountain expressions of intention to do something.

Use of Elizabethan terms—mountaineers said "afeared" instead of *afraid;* "chaw" instead of *chew;* "drap" instead of *drop;* "pert" instead of *lively;* "tetchy" instead of *sensitive;* "titch" instead of *touch;* "sight" and "power" instead of *much* or *a lot;* "nigh" instead of *near;* "plunder" instead of *goods* or *possessions;* "franzy" instead of *frenzy;* "against" and "afore" instead of *before;* "contrary" instead of *spite;* "betwixt" instead of *between;* "nary" and "airy" instead of *neither* and *either;* "heap" instead of *many;* "puny" instead of *sickly;* "misery" instead of *pain;* and I am certain everyone who gave any thought to it would come up with several more examples.

Mountain derivatives of common words—these include "agin" for *against,* "atter" for *after,* "bar" for *bear,* "bresh" for *brush,* "borry" for *borrow,* "cheer" for *chair,* "chimbley" for *chimney,* "contrarious" for *contrary,* "deef" for *deaf,* "disremember" for *don't remember,* "flustrated" for *frustrated,* "garding" for *garden,* "gal" for *girl,* "het" for *heated,* "intrust" for *interest*, "jest" for *just*, "jubious" for *dubious*, "jine" for *join*, "kin" for *can*, "kiver" for *cover*, "keerless" for *careless*, "kittle" for *kettle*, "pitcher" for *picture*, "quar" for *queer*, "skeerse" and "skeersely" for *scarce* and *scarcely*, "spile" for *spoil*, "sich" for *such*, "shet" for *shut*, "tuther" for the *other*, "tollible" for *tolerable*, "vittles" for *victuals*, "wal" for *well* and "yaller" for *yellow*.

Original mountain words and terms—foremost among these is "varmints" for minks, weasels, skunks and other small woods animals, and they also include "d'reck'ly" for immediately, "tote" for carry, "poke" for bag, "old ned" for fat pork, "sluggin' " for valise or suitcase, "tight-scrooghin' " for difficult, "anti-godlin' " for crooked or not straight, "all-overs" for nervousness, and "lit a shuck" for left or departed.

Perhaps the best known of all mountain words and most used by "furriners" when making fun of Mountaineers is "hit" which is used for *it*. Few who laugh know, however, that "hit" is the Old Anglo-Saxon neuter form of the pronoun "he" and thus is a legacy of ancient culture rather than a manifestation of contemporary ignorance.

But the most colorful and picturesque characteristic of mountain speech is that it is replete with original mountain expressions which are distinguished by dramatic hyperbole and graphically descriptive metaphor. Many of them long since have found their way into universal American usage, and their users are unaware of their mountain origin.

Some notable examples are as follows:
"Nothin' will do him but . . ."
"Rode hard and put up wet."
"Sick as a dyin' calf in a hailstorm."
"Purty as a speckled pup under a red waggin."
"His mouth ain't no prayer book."
"Vomit up shoe soles."
"On the down go."
"Rough as a cob."
"Borned tired and raised lazy."

"Get shed of."
"I'm a fool about . . ." (meaning to like something)
"Plum dumfoundered."
"Plum tuckered."
"All tuckered out."
"Let's go halvers."
"Purty rough kentry."
"Shore 'nuff."
"Stay a spell."
"Pore folks."

Equally colorful as the language are the names of places in the Mountains. In my home county of Towns there is Bugscuffle, Bear Meat, Hog Creek, Sunnyside, Fodder's Creek, Sulkey's Gap, Shake Rag and Upper and Lower Hightower. And in the neighboring counties of Union and Rabun there are Warwoman, Bugsnort, Racepath Creek, Tiger, Bad Creek, Worse Creek and Devil's Branch. Shirley was born near Granny Squirrel Gap and grew up in Rail Cove. Hanging Dog and Raw Dough are nearby, as are Shootin' Creek and Chunky Gal Mountain.

The names of the mountains and valleys include Three Sisters, Double Knob, Crow Gap, Dismal Mountain, Sunset Rock, Blood Mountain, Bat's Cave, Cupid's Falls, Bleeding Heart Meadow and Enchanted Mountain.

Every man in the mountains and many of the women had nicknames. Arnold Keys of Young Harris was the one who gave them to me and most of my contemporaries. There was Goat Jenkins, Magpie Plott, White Wolf Nichols, Fed-Face Gordon, Square-Jaw Stephens, Red-Eye Roland, Dude Dean, Mole Daniels, Mouse Keys and Madam Chiang Chastain.

I had two nicknames—"Drew" and "Zip"—both related to baseball.

"Take Two Drew," my second-base partner, Arnold Keys, used to say.

There was awhile that I was known around the "loafers' bench" as "Cave Man" because I wouldn't get a haircut.

That follows me to this day because my wife, Shirley, uses it on me when I am overdue for a trip to the barber.

And my office staff was convulsed with merriment not long ago when an old classmate who had moved to the West Coast came to Atlanta and called on the phone to speak to "Zip" Miller.

All of which should go to prove that you can take the barefoot boy out of the mountains—and even put shoes on him—but you can't take the mountains out of the boy.

# VII

# Mountain Victuals

*Why has our poetry eschewed*
*The rapture and response of food?*
*What hymns are sung, what praises said*
*For home-made miracles of bread?*

*Food and Drink*
Louis Untermeyer

With all her talents, my mother showed little interest in food or the art of mountain cooking. Physical labor appealed more to her than sweating over a hot stove. To her, eating was a physical necessity which was to be satisfied in the easiest and most expeditious manner possible.

It was my good fortune, however, to have an aunt who not only was an excellent cook but also was married to a man with a hearty appetite who came from one of the pioneer families of Towns County. To keep a happy home and a contented husband, she was compelled to learn all the mountain ways of preparing food.

Euzelia Bryan was my mother's half-sister. She had come to YHC as a student and married the star athlete, a local man named Hoyle Bryson who, after a brief stint as a professional baseball player, returned with his wife to Young Harris and for a while lived upstairs in our home.

89

Later they built their own home next door to Birdie's house, where they still live. I ate supper with "Phoebe," as I called her, at least three or four times a week, and hers are the only real, honest-to-goodness meals I recall having as a boy.

Shirley's mother, Beatrice Carver, was an even better cook than Phoebe—she also married a man who wanted food prepared in the manner and style of his mountain forebears. "Mama Bea" could prepare a mountain meal that was second to none.

We always had plenty of food in the mountains. We grew and prepared most of it for ourselves, or it grew wild and we learned how to take nature's wonders and utilize them just as the Indians had done earlier.

Every mountain family had its own garden, and the planting, gathering, canning and drying of its produce required the involvement of everyone in the family. Usually more than enough was produced each spring and summer to last through the following winter with plenty to share with those who might not have enough. Even today mountaineers still plant more than they need and share it with children, grandchildren and "family" who have left the mountains for the cities. Many are the times Shirley and I have visited "Mama Bea" and returned loaded down with fresh vegetables or, in the winter, canned goods.

Opening a jar of "Mama Bea's" home-grown, canned green beans for supper would always make me homesick for a summer supper in the mountains.

It is amusing to me to find that certain strata of society regard our everyday mountain eats as "delicacies." I am more than a little envious of those people who had the foresight to compile cookbooks of mountain recipes and make money telling "furriners" how to make cracklin' bread and red-eye gravy.

Mountain folks respected food. They knew the necessity of planting more than was needed for one season and putting it up because the next season might not yield as much. They also took the wild and natural foods sparingly, remembering that natural foods should not be depleted if those plants were to be used again or if game were to reproduce itself. They took and killed only what was needed.

While individuals grew much of their own food, mountain communities also had a communal approach to food processing. One family would have a corn mill and grind corn for everyone else. Another family would make sorghum syrup and supply the remainder of the community. My ancestors were big syrup-makers.

Payment for food not produced at home was made mostly by bartering or sharing on a percentage basis. The syrup-maker, for example, might keep three gallons for every ten he made for someone else. The miller would receive a specified number of "toddicks" of meal for each bushel of corn he ground.

There were two corn mills in our valley. Both were run by large waterwheels which turned the huge millstones which ground the corn between them. Andy Bryson, who was Hoyle's father and one of Young Harris' pioneers, operated one. The other was about two miles away at Townsend's Mill operated by Gus Townsend, who married my cousin Fanny. I've spent much time at each place on grinding days and enjoyed eating the meal raw and still warm from grinding as it poured through the hopper to be caught in pans, "pokes" or whatever containers the owners of the corn had brought for that purpose.

Children learned early about nature's wonders by gathering berries and fruits. Parents, using psychology without realizing it, made these gathering tasks seem like fun, and some of my fondest childhood memories are those of picking blackberries with other people to keep you company while you worked. Even the sharp and stinging briars and the heat did not seem as bad when everyone was joking and singing while they picked. One didn't have to be too old to learn the difference between ripe berries and those not yet ready for picking. It was simply a matter of taste!

I cannot recall my first taste of sassafras tea, the drink brewed from the root of the sassafras tree which grows in the mountains. Once dug and dried, the roots are put in a kettle, covered with water and boiled until the liquid turns a rich red color. The tea can be drunk either hot or cold and sweetened to taste, and the same roots can be used over and over again and also have a pleasant, candy-like taste when chewed.

Sassafras tea is believed by many mountain old-timers to have medicinal value and is taken as a spring tonic. The Indians also used it as medicine, and in the seventeenth century shiploads were sent to Europe for use as a cure-all. When it failed to cure all ailments, however, the Europeans lost their faith in it.

Early spring often is called "green-up" time in the mountains. People go out then and gather wild greens, such as "poke sallet" and field cress or "cresses" as it is called. A few years ago, when the song "Poke Sallet Annie" was popular, it was amazing to learn how many people, particularly the younger ones, had no idea what "poke sallet" was or did not know what "pickin' a mess" meant.

The meaning of the word "mess" as used in the mountains is something one either knows or doesn't because it is impossible to define it. When you pick a "mess" there is a lot of it, and when your mama cooks up a "mess" there is going to be enough for everyone, including any unexpected and uninvited guests.

"Poke sallet" is the young shoots of the pokeberry and is similar to turnip greens. The younger the shoots are, the better; and, after they are gathered, they must be boiled all day to remove the pokeberry poison.

After the boiling, the "poke sallet" usually is cooked in a skillet and seasoned with bacon or ham drippings. Sometimes it is served with boiled eggs and some folks stir raw eggs right into the "poke sallet" while it is cooking in the skillet. "Poke," as some call it, also can be served like any other vegetable and, like most greens, is good with cornbread and the "pot likker" from the greens. Another recipe calls for taking the tender stems, cutting them up and frying them, after which they taste very much like fried okra. Phoebe could cook excellent fried "poke sallet," and it was one of my favorites.

Every Easter the Bryson family would go "ramp" hunting in the woods, and many times I would go with them. Ramps are similar to wild green onions, although leafier, and their smell can most charitably be described as horrible. You can fry them in lard or scramble them in eggs; and, after eating them, the smell stays on one's breath for days. One of the quickest ways to become a social outcast is to go into a crowd after a meal of ramps. The only way the non-eater can protect himself is either to run or to eat some himself.

Other wild food was available if one knew where to look for it.

Chestnuts were plentiful until a blight hit these hardy trees in the early 1900's; and their smaller cousins, the chinquapins, covered a hill near my home. In the early fall I spent many an afternoon gathering these dark and shiny little nuts. The hull, like that of a chestnut, was prickly and one had to be careful getting them out. But the effort and the pricks were worth it because they are delicious raw, boiled or roasted. One also could find hazelnuts down by the creek and wild plums in many places. And, of course, there were the persimmons, which are a story in themselves.

A large persimmon tree grew next door in Carter Berry's pasture, and while going to get the cows late in the afternoon, the boys would dare one another to eat the fruit while it was still green.

The fruit is thousands of years old. DeSoto, hitting them at the right season, called them prunes. It must turn an orange color before being edible, and this usually occurs after the first frost. To eat it before is to invite the worst taste imaginable and to give your mouth the sensation of being turned wrong side out or "wrongsideoutards" as we called it. (I was in college before I knew it wasn't one word.)

In nearby Cherokee County, North Carolina, there is a creek named Puckermouth Creek. Undoubtedly, persimmons grew nearby and an Indian who ate them too soon named the creek.

Once ripe, however, persimmons are very good to eat and go well with squirrel. Some people make puddings, a kind of syrup and jelly from them. They also can be used in making a sweet bread. Persimmon brandy is a rare beverage which once was recommended by Zeb Vance, a North Carolina mountain man who was elected United States Senator, as a tonic for long-winded orators. Starving Confederate soldiers used the seeds to make a substitute for coffee.

"Pot likker," for the benefit of those benighted souls who don't know, is the savory blend of cooking water, vegetable juices and stock from meat used for seasoning that combines in the pot when greens, beans, peas, cabbage or other vegetables are cooked, but is most often associated with greens. Most people eat it by crumbling a piping hot piece of cornbread and pouring the "pot likker" over it.

That soupy hot dish is some good eatin'! Some people are too young or somehow never heard about the classic debate between the self-styled country boy, Huey P. Long, and the fastidious arbiter of social graces, Emily Post, about the etiquette of eating cornbread and "pot likker." But if it is all right for city slickers to dunk their doughnuts in their coffee, then there should be nothing wrong with mountain folks sopping "pot likker."

"Sopping" is an art perfected by mountain people.

The dictionary says "sop" means to "drench, to absorb, to soak in." In the mountains "sopping" involves a piece of bread and is most often done at breakfast.

Highlanders dunk hot biscuits in steaming cups of

coffee and call it "sopping." Much like businessmen and their doughnuts, it takes a deft hand to dunk the biscuit just far enough into the coffee and pop it in the mouth before it totally disintegrates in the coffee cup.

It is recommended that beginning "soppers" dip the biscuit only half an inch or so—and do it very quickly—until they get the timing right. For the benefit of the devotees of Miss Post, it should be pointed out that the entire biscuit never is completely submerged and the fingers never touch the coffee. That would be uncouth!

"Sopping" butter and syrup is another precise mountain technique. It is done by taking a helping of butter, covering it well with syrup and blending it with a fork to the consistency of thick cake batter. Then the biscuit is broken in half and dipped into the mixture.

As with biscuits and coffee, it takes a delicate hand to "sop" syrup and butter right. It is not uncommon to hear an old pro tell a beginner, "You ain't doin' that right." The master of this fine art always finishes his biscuit and syrup and butter simultaneously—with equal servings on each bite.

A "syrup-sopping" contest is held each year in Blairsville with some contestants eating more than two dozen biscuits and coming out even every time.

Breakfast always was a hearty meal in the mountains. Everyone believed that the man who put away a good breakfast worked better, lived longer and never "went to fat."

Breakfast always included hot homemade biscuits and ham or sausage or both. Both Phoebe and "Mama Bea" often cooked fried squirrel or rabbit, and it was not uncommon to have fried chicken or ribs for breakfast.

These main courses were accompanied by sweet potatoes, hominy and grits. Mama Bea often had fried creamed corn. Her homemade biscuits always were drowning in butter and were huge ones which she jokingly called "cat-heads," a term of derision applied in some quarters to biscuits which were heavy, lumpy and hard.

Biscuits always were eaten with jams and jellies on top. Jellies were "put up" in the summer from blackberry, strawberry, apple, peach, plum, raspberry and elderberry crops. All made great jellies and jams.

Sorghum (often pronounced "soggum") syrup was made from sorghum cane which was smaller and made stronger and more pungent syrup than sugar cane. Some folks called it molasses but that was technically a misnomer.

Sorghum cane was taken to the mill in the fall of the year, and the making of syrup from it became almost a ritual autumn festival.

For years after the War Between the States and during the Great Depression, many Southerners, and particularly mountaineers, used sorghum syrup to sweeten coffee and other dishes. There are a number of people, like "Tennessee" Ernie Ford, who maintain coffee tastes better when sweetened with sorghum syrup than with refined sugar.

The soil where the cane is planted is very important to the resulting quality of syrup. The soil in the bottomlands of Towns and Union Counties is peculiarly well suited for it.

Planting time is the last two weeks in May so that the harvest will be in the early fall immediately before the first frost.

"Stripping" the cane is one of the hardest jobs in farming. This is done by pulling the tight, fuzzy leaves which have very sharp edges from around the joints of the cane stalk and cutting the red seed pods off the top of the stalk. Then the stalks are cut off at the base and taken as quickly as possible to the mill so the juice won't dry out.

There the stalks are fed into rollers which usually are rotated by a horse or mule pulling the operating tongue or lever in a circle. The green juice thus squeezed out of the cane goes through a burlap bag into a barrel, is strained again and put into a kettle or compartmented pan. Dark foam forms on the top of the juice as it begins to boil, and this is skimmed off with a long-handled skimmer and thrown away unless some old moonshiner takes it to make his liquor sweeter. The juice is cooked for about four hours, and it changes color and thickens as it boils. Then it is strained, poured out into a large metal container to cool and afterwards is "put up" in quart jars or metal syrup buckets. It takes about ten gallons of cane juice to make one gallon of syrup.

Honey made an excellent sweetener and tasted good on hot biscuits, too. Some mountain folks like it and sorghum syrup over cornpone.

Shirley's father, Luke Carver, always has worked with honey bees and has a dozen or more hives. She has helped with the honey as long as she can remember and, now that "Mama Bea" is gone, has inherited the job of putting up the honey after Luke "robs the bees."

September is usually the time to harvest the sourwood honey, and the process is a sight to behold. Luke puts on his mesh veiling and puffs some smoke from his bee smoker into the front of the hive. This, too, is a fine art. Too much smoke makes the bees irritable and increases the chances of getting stung; but exactly the right amount causes the bees to fill themselves with honey and hence become more amicable and less apt to do combat with the "robber."

Luke always approaches from the side of the hive. Operating from the front interferes with the bees' line of flight, and that is another thing that makes them angry. After removing the top of the hive, he removes the outside comb and then separates the others with a hive tool, smoking gently and being careful not to crush the bees. The bees that cling to the comb are brushed off with a paint brush. Enough honey is left for the bees to survive until the following spring when production of it resumes.

Wild game such as rabbits, squirrels, quail and turkey made good eating. It was a real treat to have venison at the Brysons' because this was before deer became plentiful as they are now. Also, raccoon and opossum were eaten when Hoyle caught them. But, truthfully, I never cared for them nor the ground hogs Luke often would catch and called "whistle pigs."

Both Phoebe and "Mama Bea" knew how to get the "wild" taste out of some meat with various herbs, and they produced some mighty tasty entrees which would be worthy of a gourmet restaurant's menu today.

The domestic animals we raised ourselves provided most of our meat. Almost everybody kept hogs and on cold winter days when the temperatures were below freezing, we would join together to butcher one or more. The fresh meat that could not be cured in the smokehouse was shared immediately with all the neighbors and relatives.

Hog-killing time was almost a festival occasion in the mountains, and certainly it had many aspects of a ritual with friends, relatives and neighbors swapping off their services to each other on successive weeks in the early winter in getting the job done. While it was not a time for the squeamish or the faint of heart or stomach, it was one of camaraderie and good eating for those not turned off by the gory details of butchery or such unfastidious chores as the rending of the "chitlins."

Killing, cleaning and cutting up the hog was an all-day job which began with the building of the fires and boiling of the water with the freezing first light of dawn and finished with the grinding and stuffing of the sausage and the hanging of the dressed meat in the smokehouse in the failing light of dusk.

Once the water was boiling in a half dozen or so borrowed cast-iron washpots, half the men would proceed to dispatch the hog while the remainder poured the boiling water into a huge barrel usually half buried on a slant in the ground as near as possible to the hogpen. The animal would be fed some corn to distract him while the owner dropped him with one well-aimed shot from a 22-caliber rifle or a pistol or a blow to the head with the blunt end of an ax. When he fell, one of the men would jump into the pen and slash his throat with a razor-sharp butcher knife so all the blood could run out before it congealed.

When the bleeding was complete the men would knock down the side of the pen, manhandle the carcass onto a board or mule-pulled drag and pull it to the vat where, using a singletree and a block and tackle, they would maneuver it into the bubbling water. If the barrel were not large enough to immerse the entire hog, the process would have to be repeated for the other end. Once the scalding was completed, the carcass would be lifted high by the hind legs and the scraping would commence until all the hair was removed and the skin was smooth and shiny white.

While still hanging, the carcass would be disemboweled with great care being taken not to puncture any of the internal organs and thus taint or disflavor the meat. Pans from the kitchen were ready to receive such delicacies as the heart, liver, pancreas or "melt" as it was known by some and for those who relished them the lungs or "lights." The small intestines were placed in a washtub and carried a distance downwind where they would be rended and cleaned, usually by the womenfolks, and prepared to be chitlins or use as sausage casings if the owner of the hog could not afford storebought ones.

The empty carcass would then be stretched out on a cutting table made of boards suspended across sawhorses and the "cutting up" would begin—first the head and then the hams, shoulders or "picnics," belly and sides, ribs and backbone. When the ribs and backbone were reached, the tenderloin was removed, it being what we would know today as the center of the porkchop, and taken by one of the watching children to the kitchen where it would be fried and served with hot biscuits and milk pan gravy for the traditional "hog-killing day" dinner as noon meals were called in the mountains. Being very perishable and because of a lack of refrigeration, the tenderloin always was consumed on the day of the hog-killing, and I was well into my teens before I learned people ate pork chops at any other time.

All of the pieces were trimmed closely and carefully, and the lean trimmings were piled in pans for sausage and the fat placed in a washtub to be boiled down for lard and cracklin's, usually that same afternoon by the women. The hams were rubbed with salt and spices and hung in the smokehouse as were the shoulders unless they were to be used in the sausage, in which case they were cut into grinding-size chunks of lean. The head, after the brains were removed for serving with eggs for the next day's breakfast, and the feet were saved for use by the wife of the owner in making "sousemeat" or "head cheese" after being boiled to release the gelatin which would hold it together when fashioned by her into a loaf.

The belly fat and, unless it was to be smoked for bacon, the streak-o-lean of the sides were cut into slabs and salted down for curing in the bins in the smokehouse. The chitlins, after being cleaned and rinsed and re-rinsed, were soaked in a weak lye solution if they later were to be fried and eaten as the mountain delicacy they were regarded to be or were stretched out and cut into stuffing lengths if they were to be used to hold the sausage.

The ribs and backbone were cut up and divided among the participants in the "killing" and were destined to be barbecued or boiled as meals for their families during the coming week.

By that time it was midafternoon and the sausage mill was brought out and the grinding, seasoning and stuffing of the meat began. This was where the children came in as they were pressed into service to turn the handles of the grinders. It was hard, muscle-numbing work and every now and then some overly weary youngster would get careless and get a finger caught in the mill.

Usually two kinds of sausage were mixed—extra hot with a lot of pepper for the menfolks and a milder version for the womenfolks. Once stuffed in the casings or chitlins, both ends were tied and they were rubbed with salt and spices and also hung in the smokehouse to cure with the hams and bacon. Since they cured faster than the others, they were the first of the cured meat to be available for the table later in the winter. But for those who liked their sausage strong, the last and most-dried-out links were by far the best, even if they did have to be soaked before they were soft enough to be cooked.

My knowledge of hog-killing came mostly from participating in the occasion at other people's houses. We tried raising a hog once, but with Birdie's casual approach to cooking, we simply didn't have enough "slops" to fatten a hog and we had to content ourselves with the gifts of our relatives and neighbors when they killed theirs.

It saddens me when I think that my children and grandchildren will never know the excitement of or gain the knowledge of life that comes from participating in syrup-making or hog-killing.

Today the term "smokehouse" usually refers to a storage shed behind a dwelling house, but it used to be literally a "smokehouse." When I was a boy smokehouses had dirt floors with a hole dug in the center in which a fire was built. The dressed hams and sometimes the shoulders, bacon and sausage would then be hung above the fire to smoke. Other meats were preserved by drying and the pork bellies or "fatback" would be packed in salt in big bins or boxes around the side of the smokehouse. Usually hogs were smoked and beef was dried.

I never ate beef as a boy. In fact, I had not eaten steak until I joined the Marine Corps. There were two reasons: Birdie was not a beef-eater and also, at that time, beef was a rich man's food. The meat I ate was pork—sausage, backbone or ribs—and chicken. Then there was the wild game at "Phoebe's."

We did not have an icebox or refrigerator until I was nine years old. In the winter the milk was kept on the kitchen windowsill or in a jar lowered into the well. We never owned a cow but got two quarts of milk from Kitty Bryson, who lived across the pasture back of our house. One of my chores was to go get the milk each evening. I would take two quart fruit jars and pick up two others filled with warm milk. By morning the thick cream would have risen to the top and have filled about half the jar.

From cow's milk came butter, buttermilk and, occasionally, even ice cream. Many a kid got stuck with the task of churning butter when he would rather have been romping through the woods.

Butter churns were usually about three feet tall and nine inches in diameter, were made of wood or clay and looked very much like large pitchers. Butter and buttermilk were made by taking freshly strained milk and setting it in a warm spot, usually by the fireplace in winter, until the clabber formed. Then the dasher, which was an "X"-shaped plunger, was inserted through the small hole in the churn lid and pushed up and down by the usually reluctant churner until the butter "came." If the clabber was thin or the weather too cold or too hot, it could take up to an hour or more for the butter to "come." The butter floating on top was dipped from the churn and pressed into a wooden mold for squeezing out the excess liquid and for shaping. What was left was buttermilk which was poured into jars and put in the well to cool. There is no finer way to quench a summer thirst than with a glass of buttermilk flecked with butter flakes.

Many mountain dishes came straight from the Cherokee Indians. It is a well-documented fact that the white man was introduced to corn by the Indians.

The Cherokees passed down many delicate dishes. One is yellowjacket soup which sounds only a little more appetizing to most whites than the traditional Cherokee dishes of blood pudding, lye dumplings and slick-go-downs (which were boiled mushrooms served with corn-meal mush).

Pumpkins also were widely used by the Cherokees. Many people think pies and jack-o'-lanterns are the only things made from pumpkins. But mountaineers used them to make pumpkin bread, pudding, molasses and butter. The latter is much like apple butter and makes a delicious spread for hot biscuits.

Bread is made by stewing the pumpkin and combining it with cornmeal or flour and salt all worked into a dough. Pudding is made by boiling the pumpkin just right. Molasses was made by cooking the pumpkin in a large quantity of water for a long time, straining it and then reducing the pulp to a thick syrup by boiling. Some ingenious folks even knew a recipe for making pumpkin whiskey.

Birdie used to say, "Bread is the staff of life," and we had plenty of it of all kinds at our house. As to the Indians, corn was a staple for mountaineers and their uses of it were infinite. Cornbread was eaten in some mountain homes three times a day. Many purists claimed that, to be any good, it had to be made from meal that was water ground and cooked in an iron skillet.

Ashcakes, johnny cakes, cracklin' bread, corn muffins, cornsticks, spoonbread, mushbread, egg bread, corn dodgers, battercakes, cornpone—all are mountain varieties of cornbread.

As a vegetable dish, there was corn-on-the-cob, creamed corn, whole kernel corn, corn pudding and all kinds of corn casseroles. Probably the most infamous and profitable of all uses is corn whiskey which most often is identified with the mountains.

The bottomland in Towns County, what there is of it, is very rich and yields more bushels of corn per acre than nearly any other county in Georgia.

Flour was another staple. It was made by grinding wheat. What bread was not made with cornmeal was made with flour. Those mouth-watering breakfast biscuits were made from a dough made with flour, salt, soda, buttermilk and shortening.

Flour also was used for dumplings. Chicken and dumplings is a mountain favorite. Dumplings are made by dropping small strips of dough into boiling water and stewing it into a soupy concoction, mixed with finely chopped chicken pieces and sometimes vegetables and herbs.

Chicken could be battered and fried, boiled, baked, stewed or broiled. The livers, heart, gizzards and brains made good eating to those who liked them. Chickens also provided the eggs which were a dish by themselves. Eggs were and are an essential ingredient in most cakes and many breads (some cooks add them to cornbread and some do not). Eggs also are used to batter many frying meats, especially chicken. (Luckily we didn't know too much about cholesterol when I was growing up.)

Methods of cooking are as important as the foods used in the mountains. Unless it was cooked in a black iron skillet, cornbread was not really cornbread to most mountain people. Sweet potatoes, to be really tasty, had to be cooked in a dutch oven placed in hot coals.

Even though nutritionists tell us today that vegetables should be cooked only a short time to retain all their nutritional value, few mountain old-timers would agree. "Vegetables just can't cook long enough," I've heard some mountain cooks say, and I still don't relish my string beans, carrots or cabbage crisp. In the first place, you don't get "pot likker" with quick boiling; and, in the second place, vegetables really aren't tasty until cooked limp and completely permeated by the seasoning of the meat with which they are boiled.

# VIII

# Moonshine and Bootleggers

*John Barleycorn was a hero bold,*
*Of noble enterprise,*
*For if you do but taste his blood,*
    *'Twill make your courage rise,*
*'Twill make a man forget his woe;*
    *'Twill heighten all his joy.*

*John Barleycorn*
Robert Burns

Until recent years moonshining was as much a part of the mountain way of life as syrup-making and hog-killing. In fact, mountaineers thought of it as an extension of the harvest and a means of preserving some of the fruits of their spring and summer labors for the long, cold months of winter. It was a part of their Anglo-Saxon and Anglo-Celtic heritage, and no one thought any more of making whiskey than grinding corn and wheat into meal and flour or burying turnips in a root cellar and sweet potatoes in a hill. It was a skill which was handed down with pride from father to son for generations.

Although its commercial and extralegal aspects have been romanticized and sensationalized by contemporary fiction and motion pictures, its role in mountain life prior to the nation's ill-fated experiment with prohibition was a routine and accepted activity in which most families participated either by producing or bartering. It did not become a significant business until the Volstead Act made it profitable to take the risks entailed in trying to outwit and outrun the "revenuers" in marketing "white lightnin' " in the thirsty towns and cities of the flatlands.

Old-timers never understood the preoccupation of their "givermint" with trying to "bust up" their stills, and those who were caught and imprisoned never felt any stigma among their peers for their alleged transgressions. To the contrary, it was a source of pride in some families that their fathers and sons "took turns" in going to jail as the price for their continued engagement in what to them was a legitimate enterprise. To the mountain mind there certainly was never any element of the racketeering of the Capones and other hoodlums of the cities in doing what the men of the mountains always had done.

In recent times, of course, this has changed. Most mountain families do not engage in moonshining any more, and those who do, for the most part, are a breed apart from their ancestors to whom making whiskey was a personal, custom-sanctioned activity that was incidental to their total livelihood and not a calculated, law-breaking enterprise. Many of those who now make their living this way are not mountain people at all, but outsiders who have chosen the mountains as the best place to carry on their illicit operations, and most of the others are bankrolled in their activities by underworld elements in the cities who make all the profits and take few of the risks.

Most of the stories we read about big still operations today are about mass-production facilities set up with great cunning and at considerable expense in and around the metropolitan areas by slick operators who see the mountains only when they go on vacation. There is as much difference in their operations and traditional mountain moonshining as between the dark and bright sides of the moon.

My story is about the mountain moonshiner and not the cold-blooded, modern illegal whiskey-maker who has perverted and sullied the colorful mountain art of producing spirits for home consumption.

I grew up with mountain moonshiners and understood them. I had classmates who worked at stills and some of them were among my best friends. While I was winning awards for debating at Young Harris College, some of these friends were "hauling liquor" in their 1940 Fords.

Shirley's father, Luke Carver, was a sheriff and law enforcement officer in North Carolina for many years and had to arrest some of the more flagrant moonshiners. However, he was their friend just as I was and understood that most were in a business into which they had been born and that their skill was one which had been handed down for many generations.

Two of my friends were Theodore King and Jack McClure.

Once when I was on the Board of Pardons and Paroles, an assistant brought a request for a commutation to my desk with the remark, "This is the most unusual I've ever seen, but he says he knows you."

The name on the file was Theodore King or "Thee" as I called him or "Doc King" as he called himself. I told the assistant I knew him all right because he had been my friend all of my life and had been in and out of trouble with the law all of his life.

Well, "Thee" had petitioned for release from prison on the grounds that he was needed at the Georgia Mountain Fair held every August in Hiawassee to run the old-fashioned liquor still which so fascinated the tourists and visitors. He had operated this popular exhibit for the Fair from its inception, having been given the job on the solemn oath that he had "reformed" and no longer was in the business himself.

Unfortunately, "Thee" had become "unreformed" between Fairs and had gotten caught and sentenced to prison. He had heard I was on the Board and appealed to me for clemency because he knew I knew he was a favorite with the fair-goers and that it just would not be the same if he were not there to enthrall the gawking city-slickers with his routine as a great story teller, prevaricator and natural wit and to pose with the still for the snapping cameras.

I denied the request, not because I didn't love "Thee" or because he wasn't one of the Fair's biggest drawing cards, but because in his request he made a statement that I knew to be another tall tale.

"Thee" had said: "I am needed because I am the only person in Towns County who knows how to operate a liquor still."

That simply was not true as I, of all people, knew; and, while I could have disqualified myself from acting on the case and left it to my colleagues, with great sadness I denied the request because there really were no extenuating circumstances to warrant its approval.

So the Mountain Fair had to get along without "Thee" that year.

Jack McClure was the John Wayne of our section. A bear-like man who weighed about 250 pounds, he wore a Stetson hat, and his shirt was always, even in winter, unbuttoned with a mat of reddish-gray hair exposed. He was loved, hated, respected and feared, depending upon the experience one had had with him.

I loved and respected him, and it was a sad day when I drove from Atlanta to Brasstown Church for his funeral a few years ago. I had visited him on his deathbed a few weeks earlier and had come away shocked and depressed at how his massive body had been reduced to skin and bones by the ravages of cancer.

I did not fear him as many people did. As a boy I knew this almost-legendary figure and recall Mr. Erwin sometimes generating discussion in his class by posing the question, "Who do you think would win in a fight, Jack McClure or Hoyle Bryson?"

Once while I was a college student, I was helping referee a high school basketball game in the Hiawassee

Gymnasium. My refereeing partner, in a controversial decision, forfeited the game and awarded the victory to the opposing team. Jack McClure was there, as he was for every game, sipping from the bottle he always carried discreetly in a brown paper bag.

As I was leaving the gym, a hairy arm like a tree trunk blocked the door. It was Jack McClure who said softly:

"You're not going to leave just yet, Son."

Ashen-faced and trembling, I sat down and did not leave until Jack had departed.

The next morning as I was walking from home to the campus and was passing the store, Jack crossed the street and spoke to me. He explained he had wanted me to stay because he thought the game might be continued. He told me he admired my refereeing, thought my mother was a hard worker and knew I must be all right, too.

From that day until his death, Jack McClure was a close friend and ally. His heart was as big as the rest of his frame. He was the first to give to any charitable cause and always gave the most. His presence at box suppers and cake walks, which were used frequently to raise money for charities, insured their success and, at baseball games, he always put five dollars in the hat when it was passed. Many sick and needy persons had food and health care because of his generosity, and he loaned money to anyone who wanted to borrow it and seldom was repaid.

Because of him, I cannot and never will think ill of mountain men who saw nothing wrong with making a little whiskey of good quality to drink themselves and to sell to their neighbors.

To understand mountain moonshining, one must understand the origin and heritage of mountain people, which I have discussed in an earlier chapter. Their forefathers brought with them the traditions and customs of Elizabethan England when they settled in mountain isolation, and those mores, including the making and consumption of spirituous liquor, remained unchanged and unquestioned for more than two centuries. Early colonists brought with them the Old World custom of drinking beer and wine, a practice in which even the Puritans aboard the Mayflower indulged, and they soon learned how to apply the distilling process with which they were familiar to make whiskey from Indian corn and rum from sugar cane and fermented molasses.

It was from the Irish among them that the term "moonshine" and the techniques of "moonshining" were derived, their native countrymen having perfected the art and the nomenclature in the misty glens and fens of Ireland during the days when the liquor tax of the English Government made smuggling of brandy, gin, whiskey and other alcoholic beverages a large and lucrative enterprise in that part of the world. The oppressive and hated Molasses and Sugar Acts which the British imposed on the colonies expanded the practice into the Americas and, at one time, John Hancock and Samuel Adams were among those engaged in profitable rum and molasses smuggling; the molasses, of course, subsequently was distilled into rum in moonshining-type operations.

So the pioneers of the Southern Mountains brought with them this background and knowledge, and it was only natural that the distilling of spirits should become an integral part of their transplanted and unchanging way of life. In fact, their existence was so insulated and their homes and settlements so isolated that they were little affected by the turmoil precipitated by the efforts of the new American government which followed the Revolution to impose an excise tax on liquor and which culminated in the brief, but intense, violence of the Whiskey Rebellion. But their experience with the British and what little they heard and felt from the United States Government left them with an ingrained distrust of governments and tax collectors, particularly as they concerned the making and consumption of whiskey and alcoholic beverages. Since they made their whiskey from the grain they had grown themselves, they regarded any tax on liquor as a tax on grain and bread and that, to them, was too unjust to be borne. And they had a strong ally in Thomas Jefferson, who called the excise tax "infernal" and one that is "hostile to the genius of a free people."

Being independent by nature, mountain people felt it was none of the "givermint's" business what they did on their own land—and certainly not where the making of moonshine for their own consumption was concerned—and that attitude continued well into the twentieth century, and vestiges of it remain today. I know that such thought persisted when I was a boy because that was one of the subjects I most frequently heard "chawed over" on my visits to the "loafer's bench."

The determined resistance of mountain men, and sometimes entire families, to the accelerated encroachments of "revenuers" during the years of prohibition was the most physical manifestation of this attitude. The swarms of government agents that were sent into the Highlands during the 1920's and 1930's to seek out and "bust up" illegal stills were met with open hostility, and sometimes pitched battles were fought over the possession of stills. The moonshiners, of course, always lost and, if they were not fast enough to avoid capture, wound up serving time in the same penitentiaries as the gangsters of New York, Chicago, St. Louis and the other big cities—the justice of which the mountaineers never understood or accepted.

In addition to making whiskey for their own consumption, mountain people also found it necessary to trade whiskey for staples and goods they could not produce for themselves—things like salt, gunpowder, medicines, tea, needles, nails and cloth. They also would use it as an item for bartering goods among themselves to get local commodities in which they might find themselves in short supply. But, as I have noted, it was not until prohibition that this native mountain product went commercial—or, in agricultural terms, became a "cash crop."

Until that time whiskey was mainly a personal and

social thing. It was carried to every community gathering and festivity, including funerals, and was freely available and consumed after outdoor church services and at house-raisings, log-rollings, quiltings, weddings, corn-huskings, christenings and especially political rallies. Through the nineteenth century and into the early part of the twentieth century, it was served at all meals and even the visiting parsons while riding the circuit partook at the homes at which they stayed overnight. There was a keg in every house and a barrel in every trading post and country store.

While people make jokes today about consuming alcohol for "medicinal" purposes and "snakebite," it was regarded and used as medicine in the mountains. It was administered for numerous ailments, including fever, rheumatism, pneumonia, food poisoning and, yes, snakebite. It was rubbed on the gums of teething babies to ease their pain and given as a tonic for growing children and a restorative for infants who were weak and frail. I have heard of country doctors using whiskey to revive unresponsive and premature babies upon birth and even "keeping them alive" on drops of whiskey until they became strong enough to take nourishment.

For obvious reasons, moonshining was a warm-weather pursuit. In the first place, the mash could not ferment in the cold; in the second place, transportation was difficult in bad weather; and in the third, and perhaps most important place, movement could be better observed by law enforcement officers when the trees were bare and tracks could be followed in the snow. So, except for the more enterprising who set up operations in caves or dug out carefully camouflaged cellars, the distilling activity was limited to the late spring, summer and early fall. Most stills were located in isolated, thickly-wooded ravines or coves alongside free-flowing streams with small waterfalls or in the shadows of remote hills through which chimneys were built to carry away the smoke in an inconspicuous manner on the other sides.

Of course, there always was some clever fellow who went his contemporaries one better, like the entrepreneur who dug a cellar under his hogpen which had a trapdoor in the floor. The floor was covered with straw on which the hogs drowsed during the day and, at night, the man and his partners chased them out and made their runs of 'shine. This gave them the further advantage of feeding the "spent" mash to the hogs, which were said to be the fattest and happiest porkers in the hollow.

Using hogs as a disposal for the leavings of still operations was a fairly common practice, and many a "revenuer" got his tip about the existence of a clandestine distillery by spotting tipsy swine. My father-in-law remembers a still operated in conjunction with a sawmill where the owners kept a herd of 100 hogs for that purpose. He said the way those pigs "wobbled around" reminded him of what he had heard, but never experienced personally, about "some of those big city cocktail parties."

Some of the moonshiners fed their "spent" mash to their cows and said they staggered a lot but gave the best and richest milk in the hills. Some of the tall tale spinners at the "loafers' bench" vowed they had had some milk that "was 100 proof" from such cows.

Such ingenuity also was exhibited in the selling of the finished product. One fellow buried a barrel under a road being built above his house with pipes running into it from the still on one side and from it into his house on the other. He installed a spigot on the house end of the pipe, and when a customer came by with his jug, he turned the tap and gravity did the rest. He probably never would have been caught except he sampled too much of his own wares one time and blabbed the secret to a "friend," who promptly told the sheriff.

Another had a window sill that could be lifted up and hid the jars in the wall, and Luke remembers searching a house he had under surveillance 15 times before discovering that it had a copper holding tank built into the wall from which the 'shine was siphoned.

Many tricks were employed by moonshiners when apprehended, like the old man who went to elaborate pains to read and examine carefully the warrant served on him when the officers came to search his house for a hidden cache which subsequently was found. Later, in court, the case had to be thrown out when it was discovered the warrant was 20 years old. Somehow the crafty fellow had switched warrants on the sheriff.

To those who are not connoisseurs, whiskey is whiskey; but to oldtime moonshiners, there are distinctions in taste and quality which vary according to the recipes used and the details of the process employed. Every moonshiner had his own special recipe which, like the commercial distilleries, he guarded jealously. Some of the recipes had been handed down for generations and originally had been brought to this country by ancestors who immigrated from Ireland.

While the recipes varied from family to family and valley to valley, the basic distilling process has not changed greatly since, as discovered by archeologists, it was first employed in ancient Mesopotamia. The North Georgia procedure, as I observed and heard about it, went like this:

The corn was selected carefully, examined and sorted by hand grain-by-grain to eliminate the kernels that were mildewed, rotted, discolored or malformed. The selected grains then were placed in some kind of container, usually a small barrel or large bucket, with holes in the bottom for drainage. Warm water was poured in and a hot, wet fabric covering placed over it. It was kept wet and warm, but not allowed to sour, until the corn sprouted enough in three or four days to make a cap on top of the container. This turned the starch of the corn into sugar or produced what was called "corn malt." "Rye malt" was made in the same way for later addition to the mixture.

Some moonshiners hastened the sprouting process by burying the corn and rye in sacks in a manure pile where the heat of spontaneous oxidation did the job faster than the warm water process, a technique which, like distilling, also stemmed from ancient times.

The sprouted corn then was dried in the sun or on the hearth before an open fire, after which it was ground into a coarse meal called "corn grits" or "chop." Most mountain families owned or bartered use of a tubmill for this process, and it was possible, if the moonshiner had a wife and several sons with strong arms, to turn out up to two bushels of ground corn a day. Great care was taken to see that the "grits" were kept absolutely dry.

"Corn grits" were converted into "sweet mash" by putting them in an oak barrel and adding hot water in the proportion called for by the recipe used, usually half a barrel of pure spring water for each bushel of ground corn. Sufficient room had to be left in the barrel to allow for the expansion that came with fermentation.

The barrel was covered and put in a warm place, either indoors or outside in the sun, and allowed to stand from three to five days. Exactly the right temperature had to be maintained and, lacking instruments for measurement, the farmer and his wife had to rely on instinct, which usually was unerring.

After the necessary time had passed, the barrel was uncovered and the contents thinned or "broken up" with warm spring water and the "rye malt" added. This formed a layer several inches thick on top of the "sweet mash," sealing the air off and the flavor in, and initiating the process of fermentation in much the same manner as yeast. (In more recent years, yeast itself has been used instead of "rye malt," thereby speeding up the fermentation process.)

The cover was replaced on the barrel and it was allowed to stand for several more days with continued care to maintain the proper temperature, during which time the "sweet mash" became "sour mash" as the sugar was changed to alcohol and carbonic acid through fermentation. When the cap "cracked," the experienced moonshiner knew by the sound that the contents were "ripe" and ready to run. The cracking sound has been described as being "like rain on a tin roof" or "old ned frying in the pan."

The elapsed time from the selecting of the kernels until the "cracking" of the cap was usually about a week, give or take a day, although more modern techniques using refined sugar and yeast speeded up the process.

It was then time to fire the still which, in most mountain family operations, was a pot-still—a copper container shaped like a large teakettle with a round lid and an extra-long spout connected to a copper-coil condenser known as the "worm." Although some of the later prohibition-era stills were huge contraptions, the average mountain still was about 35 gallons in capacity and could run 20 to 30 gallons of moonshine every four days. All of the smaller old-fashioned stills were wood fired, using mostly hardwoods cut, hauled and stacked for that purpose during the late winter weeks.

When the still was ready for operation, the "sour mash" would be dipped out of the barrels in buckets and strained into it through a cloth, a bedsheet being preferred for that purpose. It was then a tart and cloudy liquid technically known as "beer" but which the mountaineers simply called "mash."

As soon as the "mash" started to cook, the still cap or lid was put on and sealed with a putty-like paste made of flour and water. Then careful and constant attention was given to get the "mash" to the temperature of 176 degrees Fahrenheit, the temperature at which the alcohol vaporizes, and to keep it at that point. This required an even and gentle fire because if the "mash" became too hot it would scorch and ruin the batch or the steam could build up too fast and the still would explode. Most mountain men and many boys bore the scars of burns suffered because of miscalculations on this delicate point.

Because the still was sealed tight, the alcohol vapor could escape only through the "worm" which was placed in a container of cool water called a "jacket" or "cooler

Welcome to West Ga. Regional Library
dstrct4
ou checked out the following items:

The mountains within me
Barcode: 31057901998834 Due: 2007-07-11
The Penguin Quartet
Barcode: 31057904489757 Due: 2007-07-11
Bartholomew and the oobleck
Barcode: 31057902146011 Due: 2007-07-11
Yankees made simple
Barcode: 31057903198763 Due: 2007-07-11


L-HQ 2007-06-27 13:43
were helped by

barrel" and set under a waterfall or placed in an adjacent stream where cold mountain water would pour over it. As the vapor passed through the cold coil it condensed into a watery whiskey which was drawn off by a petcock or run directly into a pail, keg or jug.

The first run, called the "singlings," was a murky liquid full of impurities and excess water and if it came out too fast or was milky in appearance the still was said to be "pukin' it." Then the second run, usually made through the same still, turned it into crystal clear corn whiskey or "moonshine," "corn squeezin's" or "white lightnin' " as it was variously called. Some of the more affluent and commercial moonshiners had separate stills for each run, thereby cutting down on the time to complete both runs.

When only one still was used, as was usually the case, the pot had to be cleaned between runs, emptying out the "slop" or "spent mash" and rinsing with some of the unstrained "sour mash" to insure mellowness. The pot was wiped clean and dry with another cloth or bedsheet and the "singlings" was poured back in and the process repeated on the second run.

It was a process of judgment and intuition all the way because there were no thermometers, pressure gauges or other instruments to guide the distiller. And when the second run was completed, the moonshiner assessed the quality of his product by the "bead." He would shake a bottle of the new whiskey and if the foam rose in bubbles about the size of No. 5 shot, the proof was right; but, if it rose in big bubbles known as "frog eyes" or "rabbit eyes," it was weak and inferior.

Usually a batch would come out at between 120 and 160 proof and was potent stuff indeed. However, unless it was made with refined sugar, it would not produce a hangover. But when the commercial boys started using sugar to get twice as much liquor during prohibition, they also started turning out a product with built-in headaches; hence, the origin of the term "popskull" as applied to some of the latter-day spirits.

The development of plastic pipe has been a boon to modern-day bootleggers. Because it is relatively inexpensive and easy to lay, moonshiners are now using it to pipe cold water to stills a quarter mile or more away from mountain streams. That has added a new dimension of difficulty to the job of "revenuers" who have always looked for stills on creek banks and who now have to scour the entire countryside to find their quarry.

More colorful than the moonshiners were the moonshine haulers or blockade-runners whose legendary feats of outrunning the law to get bootleg whiskey from the mountain stills to the big city markets during the late '30's through the early '50's have been glamourized in stories, movies and songs. These forerunners of today's hot-rodders were usually young men who loved automobiles, driving them and working on them, and who could perform feats with a speeding car that even the most skillful stunt driver would be reluctant to try. When pursued by the law or confronted with a roadblock, they thought nothing of jumping a ditch, crashing through a thicket or whipping across a field in their specially-built tanker cars. They sometimes killed or maimed themselves, but they seldom were outrun or caught in conventional fashion.

One of the hauler's most spectacular and dangerous stunts was known as the Big Turnaround, which was effective if performed correctly and nearly always fatal if done incorrectly. While under chase, he would throw the car into a skid, apply the brakes lightly, jerk the steering wheel all the way around and floorboard the accelerator. As the car turned around, he aimed it straight toward his pursuer who, to avoid a head-on collision, had to take to the ditch or worse. By the time the pursuer recovered and got back on the road, if he did, the blockade runner was out of sight.

The 1940 Ford, because of its even distribution of weight, was the favorite and best-performing tanker car. It was easy to handle and when full, hugged the road and ran like a scalded dog. Some of the current liquor runners use converted Corvettes, but their performance is paled into insignificance by the feats performed with the 1940 Fords.

These Fords were operated with their original motors to which superchargers and multiple carburetors were added to enable them to cruise at speeds in excess of 100 miles per hour. They were equipped with heavy-duty tires and overriding springs and were fine-tuned to the precision of the most expensive Swiss watch. From a mechanical point of view they were a joy to behold; from a law enforcement point of view they were despised worse than the devil.

These drivers had a language all their own. "Running wet" meant carrying a load of moonshine, and "running cold" meant carrying a cargo of water to keep from attracting attention by riding too high.

The audacity of these daredevils was without parallel. They laid smoke screens and oil slicks before James Bond ever heard of them, and they dodged gunfire, crashed roadblocks and outran pursuers with an elan that would have been a credit to Batman and Robin. Many stars on the stockcar racing circuit learned their skills as or from moonshine runners.

The day of the traditional mountain moonshiner has gone the way of that of the original cowboy of the Old West; but, like the cowboy, he always will be remembered, and the memory will become more colorful and romantic with the embellishments that come with the passage of time.

# IX

# Mountain Politics

*Political democracy as it exists and practically works in America, with all its threatening evils, supplies a training school for making first-class men. It is life's gymnasium, not of good only, but of all.*

Democratic Vistas
Walt Whitman

In the foothills of the Appalachians where Georgia, North and South Carolina and Tennessee come together, some of the roughest and most unusual politics in all the nation is practiced. It is not simply a political-year pastime, but is extremely serious business that divides neighbors and sometimes even families.

Towns County, where I grew up and first participated in politics, is in the middle of this area. There, in the past and still to a degree, Democrats buy gasoline only at service stations owned by Democrats and Republicans shop only at stores owned by Republicans. Parents in Democratic families frown on their offspring marrying Republicans and vice versa.

Sharp partisan divisions go back even further than the War Between the States. Jacksonian democracy was born on the frontier from where many of the settlers came, and Old Hickory's national philosophy clashed with the sectionalism of many Southerners. It was the War, however, which set the party pattern which still exists in this mountain area.

Towns County is an excellent example. In 1861, John Corn, a Republican, refused to sign the Secession Ordinance in Georgia. A descendant, C. D. Corn, also a Republican is Probate Judge-Commissioner of Towns County today. (Towns and Union Counties are among the very few counties in which these offices are merged.)

Last names immediately tell one the party to which a person belongs. All Taylors are Democrats; all the Shooks, Republicans. Likewise the Brysons, Dentons and Plotts are Democrats, and the Corns, Garretts and Woods are Republicans.

Of course, there have been notable exceptions, the best example being the Collinses of Union County. The present Commissioner is Neal Collins, a Democrat, who defeated Republican Gene Collins by a few votes who had been e-lected by one vote over Wayne Collins, a Democrat. This is nothing new. Dr. M.D. Collins, longtime State Superintendent of Schools, was a Democrat. His brother, Dr. Norman V. Collins, was a Republican who was elected Tax Receiver without the vote of his Democratic brother.

The split in the Collins family occurred in the generation living during the War Between the States and Reconstruction.

There were probably some historical reasons for it. Like most of the frontiersmen, these hardy, self-sufficient mountaineers were not slave owners. They had little in common with the large plantation owners of the Piedmont and Coastal Plains who raised cotton and owned slaves. Hence, they were anti-secessionist and anti-Civil War. This lack of concern for the race issue extended into the recent political history of the region. Eugene Talmadge always found his most outspoken opposition in this region, partly because his longtime opponent, E. D. Rivers, had gone to

Young Harris College, but mostly because these mountaineers found his racist politics repugnant.

And, as late as the Georgia Presidential Primary of 1976, George Wallace got his fewest votes in this region.

The family split in political parties always has intrigued me, and I've asked many of my relatives about it. One knowledgeable source, who is a Democrat, told me: "It was the 'old Collinses' who were Republicans. They couldn't read or write. The ones who first learned to read and write and 'knowed better' were Democrats."

At any rate, they were divided and, on election day, party loyalty came even before food. My grandmother, Jane, a staunch Democrat, refused to vote for her own brother, "Bud" Collins, a Republican candidate for the Georgia General Assembly. He was elected anyway.

Earlier families were divided as much on the issue of the War—so much so that it was not uncommon for one brother to serve in the Confederate Army and another in the Union Army.

Vengeance Creek flows on the way to Shirley's home. It was so named because of a family that not only fought on opposing sides but even had relatives kill one another over the War issue.

When I was growing up, virtually all of our neighbors were Republicans—the Corns, Berrys and Ensleys. They were wonderful neighbors who would give you the shirt off their backs, but they would not vote in a Democratic Primary.

Although my mother was an officeholder for many years, she played very little part in the partisan politics that swirled around her. Since both sides respected her, she was the perfect person to help hold elections.

My first taste of partisan politics came immediately after I returned from the Marine Corps. I had been discharged in late August, 1956, and in November the Democrats chose me to be a "marker" in the Young Harris precinct. A "marker" is the person who gives assistance to the elderly, blind, disabled and illiterate. There were many voters in Towns County who used "markers," and both parties selected such helpers. A wrongly motivated "marker" could change the outcome of a close election by voting people differently from the way they wanted to vote. In elections where only a few votes separate the winners and the losers—which was the case in most mountain elections—one can see how crucial this could be

Indicative of how close the outcomes of these elections often were, is that my grandfather, "Bud" Miller, ran for Ordinary around the turn of the century and was defeated by two votes by "someone on the lower end of the county."

To this day virtually all local races are very close. About 40 percent of the people vote Democratic and 40 percent vote Republican, regardless of who the candidates are. The other 20 percent are known as the "floating vote." This includes independents and what is called derisively "sell-outs." Even some "sell-outs," persons who traditionally sell their vote for $5.00 to $50.00, depending upon the fierceness of the contest, will sell their vote only to one party.

There is no apathy in mountain elections. Every voter is pinpointed and each followed up religiously.

The way I was taught to prepare for an election was to take the voting list for each precinct and go over it with a knowledgeable person who lived in that district. When I represented that area in the Senate, I knew each citizen so well I could do it without help. I would go down the list putting plus signs by the names of those known to favor my candidacy, minus signs by those who opposed it and small circles by those whose views were unknown. Known as "floaters," these were the ones to whom I would pay particular attention.

I had my first taste of actually running for office in 1958. I stood outside the "law house" all day and asked Democrats to vote for me for one of three seats on the Towns County Democratic Executive Committee. This small committee of about 15 persons was very powerful because, in those days, it nominated the Democratic candidates for office rather than having them run in primaries. It was a system that had evolved to avoid the hot conflicts which developed when primaries were held and which always carried over to the November General Elections without giving the primary wounds a chance to heal. Both parties nominated this way in Towns County.

I was elected to the Committee and, before I could turn around, found myself being pushed by some for the nomination for State Representative at the age of 26 years. When the old committee met, I lost the nomination by one vote. It was a little hard to understand why the old committee, instead of the one just elected, nominated, but that was the way the chairman had ordered it. I had had my first lesson in Towns County politics.

In 1960, I was ready to try again—or, at least, I thought I was. The Georgia Senate seat at that time rotated among Rabun, Towns and Union Counties. It was Towns' time and, for that one office, a primary had to be held.

In 1958, I had been elected Mayor of Young Harris in a strange fashion. The election was held one Saturday afternoon when I had gone to Athens to attend a University of Georgia football game. When I got back about dark, someone walked up the hill and told me I had received 98 votes, which was more than anyone else, and I was the new Mayor of Young Harris.

It was an office I had not really thought about because city government was my mother's area and I knew two Millers in it would be one too many. My mother had volunteered earlier that morning to retire when someone had mentioned that they ought to have some "young blood" on the Council.

I enjoyed the work. Young Harris had had no changes in its Charter in 50 years. I wrote a new progressive one and got it adopted as local legislation by the next session of the General Assembly. Every dirt road was paved and the few paved ones were resurfaced. Business license fees were increased and, most importantly, the Council meetings were held in the "law house" at regular times, and all citizens were invited to attend. The Council had gotten in the habit of meeting at the Mayor's home whenever he wanted to call a meeting. That was hardly conducive to the "openness" in which I believed.

Young Harris did not have a police department, and, every once in a while, the mayor had to serve as a law enforcement officer. When he was sworn in to the office, he was given not only the seal and books of the city, but also a .38 Special and a blackjack.

Once a hot-rodder kept making a nuisance of himself by speeding through the little town. When I tried to approach his car, he would speed off. Finally, he did a "wheel job" right in front of my house while I was pitching baseball in the yard. I used the only weapon I had and threw the baseball at him with all my strength. It hit his side window with a thud and the smart-aleck sped off with a window broken by a mayor who literally had taken the law into his own hands!

For some time I had thought seriously about running for the Senate seat. I had chosen the Senate because I could go directly to the people to get elected and not have to rely on a committee. Also, I was determined that the people be given a chance to speak on whether they opposed the kind of politics that existed at that time with the entire Democratic Party machinery controlled by one man.

He was the chairman of the party, a former Senator and Representative and generally considered the political boss of the county.

My first step was to go to Dr. Clegg and ask if I could make the race. Dr. Clegg had been in my father's class when he had taught and served in the Senate from Union County and understood that the two could be mixed. To his credit, he did not think all politics was crooked, and he also was unhappy with the situation which prevailed in the county. In retrospect, I think he considered me a good

teacher with little chance of changing the political
structure, and he wanted me to get "running" out of my
system and get on with the business of being a professional
educator.

At any rate, he gave his approval to my candidacy,
and, early in 1960 at the age of 27, I announced for the
State Senate.

The primary was held in April, and I worked re-
lentlessly during the cold winter days and nights. I would
get up before daybreak and visit the early-rising mountain
families around Owl Creek, Scataway, Bearmeat and the
other isolated communities throughout the county. I did
not go to the homes of known Republicans who would not
vote in the Democratic Primary; but I visited every
Democratic household in the county, some of them time
and time again. Other candidates had always visited only
one or two key men in each precinct.

Similar to old ward leaders, they were relied on to get
the vote out and carry the precincts for their candidates.
They were good men, usually the heads of large families,
and took pride in their political abilities. They controlled
the patronage which usually consisted of a few State jobs
with the Highway, Revenue and Game and Fish Depart-
ments. These were still the days of the old county unit
system, and they were the men who could carry the county.

I did not ignore them, but I did not rely solely on
them, either. In fact, a few were automatically on my side,
not because they were for me but because they were
against my opponent. All I had to do was show them I had
a chance to win.

But that in itself was a difficult task. I was young and
looked even younger. I'll never forget an old-timer, looking
at my crew-cut and snorting: "You'll never be elected to
anything, Son, with your hair cut like that."

Although my mother was highly respected, she had no
political strength and there was no large group of relatives
on whom I could count. My aunt had married Hoyle

Bryson, and the Brysons were a large Democratic family who helped me.

But the biggest obstacle was that my opponent totally controlled the election machinery, and I quickly learned how important this was in a rural county.

To begin with, there was no way I officially could qualify and pay my qualification fee. My opponent was the Chairman of the Party, and the Secretary was his right-hand man. When my candidacy became known, it became impossible for me to get in touch with them. Finally, one morning while it was still dark, I got up, took my $150.00 check and drove to the Secretary's house. I knocked on the door at daylight and handed the startled man my qualifying fee.

This gave me an idea of what I was up against, but it was nothing compared to what I later ran into when every election holder was appointed by my opponent.

Campaigning had always been done through precinct leaders, as I have previously mentioned. Not only did I go around them, but I also, for the first time in county politics, used the media.

I made a speech over the radio station in Murphy, North Carolina, that covered the area. I placed ads in the county weekly. I got my friends, Lee Kirby and his son, Robert, to go with me to court being held in Hiawassee where they played a fiddle and guitar and I stood on an old rock column and made another speech. The next day I returned and gave out bags of parched peanuts to the court-goers.

This hard work paid off—not just my hard work, but that of dozens of friends who believed in me. I remember to this day the overwhelming sense of gratitude and inadequacy I felt at seeing "haulers" bring in persons who, because they were riding with my friends, voted for me. When the ballots were counted late that night, I won by 151 votes. I left the Courthouse in Hiawassee filled with grizzled mountaineers and their stories of fights, of vote-buying and of all the other "things" that had happened that day in their precincts and returned to my home where a large number of my fresh-faced students gathered outside the house and sang "For He's a Jolly Good Fellow." My 24-year old wife and my four and five-year old sons looked on in amazement, wondering into what I had gotten them and me.

The next week I published an itemized account of my campaign contributions and expenses in the county paper. The campaign cost came to a grand total of $419.00, of which my friends contributed $137.50.

I served in the last Senate before reapportionment changed its make-up completely. Known by the media as "the drunk Senate," it was composed of old-timers, many of whom had been in the General Assembly off and on under the rotation system for many years. Garland Byrd was the Lieutenant Governor and had well-known ambitions to run for Governor. Carl Sanders was the President Pro Tempore and was serving his third term, an unprecedented achievement made possible by Glascock County declining its right to rotation in order to let the Richmond Countian continue to serve.

The Legislature met amidst bitter controversy over two blacks entering the University of Georgia. Governor Vandiver had campaigned on a pledge of "No, not one," and the feeling against court-ordered integration was strong.

A reporter asked me that night before the opening day what I thought, and I replied: "Integration is not the worst thing I can think of; closing the University is the worst thing." The next day when we were sworn in, several of my colleagues took me to task for the statement, some good-naturedly, others pointedly critical.

I quickly came to love the legislative process and especially the historic old Senate Chamber. Many times I found myself in the minority, and often Erwin Mitchell, Bob Smalley and I would be the only ones supporting or opposing measures.

The issues did not concern the voters of Towns County

greatly. They were content to let their representative vote according to his best judgment. However, they did demand and expect him to be accessible at all times, and my phone rang continually about personal problems with government—local, State or Federal, it didn't matter, I was expected to help solve them. On Saturdays and Sundays when I was home from the Senate, thirty or more people would come by the house. Some would have problems; others only wanted to hear about what was going on and to express their opinions about it.

If I have any regret about the way government has changed, it is that this highly personal relationship has been altered.

As the Governor's race began to develop and Byrd withdrew as a candidate, I more and more turned my attention to aiding Sanders, whom I greatly admired and who was opposing Marvin Griffin. I learned then that one often offends his own supporters when he takes a stand for someone else.

In the early part of the campaign I appeared on a live television program with some other legislators on behalf of Sanders. As I hurriedly drove through Hiawassee the next morning to get to YHC to teach, two cars pulled in behind me. Seeing they were my friends, I stopped my car, and they told me in no uncertain terms that they didn't vote for me to be campaigning for that liberal who was running against their buddy, "Old Marv." My temper flared and I quickly informed them, as I did those who similarly criticized me 14 years later when I early supported Jimmy Carter for President, that, while I appreciated their support they did not own me, and I would support whomever I thought was best qualified.

Sanders was nominated in the Primary; but, before the General Election, the Supreme Court ruled that the Georgia Senate had to be reapportioned according to population. We were called back into special session to redraw the districts.

I had thought about running for Towns County

Representative, but, after reapportionment ended the rotation system, I decided to run for reelection to the Senate. The new district now included eight counties, and Towns was, by far, the smallest.

I again waged a personal campaign and carried every county except Habersham, the largest in the district and the home of my chief opponent in the primary. In Towns County I received, as I always have, a lop-sided number of the votes—1,235 to 17. I also managed to defeat a Republican opponent in the General Election and was one of five Senators to return to the new Senate in 1963.

Although I had liked the old Senate very much, the new Senate was much different. Leroy Johnson, the first black, had been elected, and a friendly, but intense, young man from Plains who had won a close and contested election was a member. His name was Jimmy Carter.

My experience taught me that after a close primary election, it is very important to get the warring factions together. This important lesson was put to use when Mary Hitt, a very formidable primary opponent, was persuaded to join forces against the Republican nominee for Lieutenant Governor in 1974. One of the things of which I am most proud is that in every race I have run, including even the first, past opponents became supporters in future races.

This chapter is not meant to be a long narrative of my political career. It is meant to explain the political environment from which I sprang—tough and highly partisan with elections always so close that each side works and scrambles hard for every single vote.

Mountaineers cannot understand why other state politicians do not share their concern for each and every vote. A friend of mine once visited Governor Vandiver and, being dissatisfied with the answer he had received, told the Governor pointedly: "Well, I'll tell you one thing, you'll never carry Lower Young Cane again!"

This was the same supporter who, after putting up several of my signs on telephone poles only to have them repeatedly torn down, hid in the bushes above the road. When the offender appeared to tear down the newly-replaced sign, he shot him in the rear with a shotgun which had a shell loaded with salt. That cured him of that bad habit!

Shirley's first job after we returned to Young Harris was in the County School Superintendent's office. He had been the only Democrat to survive a Republican sweep in 1956 and was, therefore, the only Democrat in a Republican Courthouse. He actually had received fewer votes than his opponent, but his opponent had not qualified with the State as required, and a contested election had followed. For several months, while the courts decided, both men sat huddled in the same little office, a reminder of the two-Governor episode some ten years earlier on the State level.

Since mountain elections always are so close, absentee ballots play an important part in each one. Generally speaking, the Democrats have the edge because they usually administer this important function. Four years ago the Office of the Towns County Registrar was burglarized, and boxes containing more than 300 absentee ballots were carried off never to be heard from again.

Reporting the returns late also was a general mountain practice a few years ago, but no longer is a common occurrence.

In 1952, a missing ballot box in Fannin County proved to be the difference in a close race for Commissioner of Agriculture, giving Phil Campbell the office over Garland Byrd.

When I first ran in 1960, there were eight precincts in Towns County. They since have been reduced to four. At that time some voting was done outdoors or in barn lofts. Once, even the back of a truck was used, and, when a fight broke out among some drunken observers, the election-holders simply drove the voting place down the road and away from the fracas.

Tate City was the smallest precinct in Towns County.

Far back in an isolated cove near Charlie's Creek, one could get to it only by driving to Rabun County and coming into it from that side of the mountain.

There were fourteen votes in Tate City, all in one family. In close elections they would be divided; in others the front runner would get all of them. In my first race, I carried Tate City eight to six.

They were all Democratic votes, however, and Republicans didn't even bother to campaign in Tate City. They would bring in the totals whenever all fourteen voted, and it was a common occurrence to hear the returns from Tate City soon after lunch on election day.

Prior to each election, I would pay a courtesy visit to Tate City to visit Arthur Young, who was the head of the clan. He jokingly referred to himself as the Mayor of Tate City. He lived in a 150-year old log cabin with a fenced-in front porch to keep the dogs and animals out. There was no electricity, and the outdoor toilet was built over a mountain stream nearby.

The reason I always enjoyed visiting Arthur was that he was a great fiddle player, and, if one could hit him just right, he would drag out a couple of homemade fiddles and play a few numbers—old tunes he had played all his life, most of which did not even have names. He would sometimes stop in the middle of one and say, "I need a little liquor to limber up my elbow." He then would either fetch out a jar or put the fiddle up, depending upon the encouragement his audience gave him.

# Folklore and Customs

*The favorite phrase of their law is*
*'a custom whereof the memory of man*
*runneth not back to the contrary.'*

*English Traits*
Ralph Waldo Emerson

Much of the heritage of the Southern Mountains is rooted in the names, customs and mythology of the Indians who were their original residents.

Indian names are commonplace in the mountains, and little thought is given to their origins by the natives today.

"Chattahoochee" is a good example. The river originates—as all who have heard Sidney Lanier's great poem, *Song of the Chattahoochee*, will remember—"Out of the hills of Habersham, and down the valleys of Hall."

Of course, Lanier was referring to the original Habersham County before other counties were created from it. Anyone who has visited Helen, Georgia, knows that this part of the river is clear, flows rapidly and is a favorite area for trout fishermen and canoeists.

If one follows Highway 75 North toward Towns County, the famous 560-mile long river becomes smaller;

and, starting up the mountain at Unicoi Gap, one crosses it at a point so narrow it can be stepped across.

It got its Indian name from "Chatta," which means "flowered," and "Ochee," which means "rocks." Anyone who has seen the house that Birdie built in Young Harris or has observed the many hues of the rocks found in mountain streams would agree that the name "flowered rocks" is appropriately descriptive.

Another famous Georgia river is the Chattooga River, which is the upper extension of the Savannah River and the eastern boundary between the extreme northeast corner of Georgia and South Carolina.

Its origin comes from the Old Indian town "Cha tu 'gi," which was located in that area. It is a variation of "Chatauga" which means "chicken." Lake Chatuge, the fine fishing lake in Towns County, also derives its name from this Indian word.

In this extreme corner of North Georgia also is found Ellicott's Rock, which was used in 1811 to establish the northeast corner of the State. It was named after the surveyor, Andrew Ellicott, who was selected, after years of boundary dispute between the states, to survey and indicate where the 35th degree of north latitude actually was. A huge boulder has an "N" on one side, indicating North Carolina, and a "G" on the other for Georgia. There now is an argument going that it is about 500 feet too far to the north.

To me, the name "Hiawassee," always has been one of the prettiest Indian sounds. "Hiawassee," which means "beautiful fawn," was a Cherokee Indian princess who fell in love with Nottley, a prince of the rival Catawba tribe, whose name meant "daring horseman." Legend has it that the Chief of the Cherokees promised Hiawassee she could wed Nottley if he could locate the place where the "waters of the east and west meet." After much searching, Nottley found it near the site of the present town of Hiawassee. But the old Cherokee Chief reneged on his promise, and Hiawassee committed suicide by jumping from a high cliff. Many years ago I wrote a long, narrative poem about this Indian legend. It is in this mountain area where the geographic divide runs with the waters draining off to the Atlantic Ocean through the Chattahoochee River on the east side and with those on the west side flowing into the Gulf of Mexico through the Little Tennessee River.

There is a Hiawassee River, a Hiawassee Lake, a Nottley River, a Nottley Lake and a Nottley Dam—the latter a TVA project built in the early 1940's.

Other Indian names well known today include Noontootla, a creek and an area in Fannin County meaning "shining water," and Nantahala River and Gorge near where Shirley grew up, meaning "middle sun." There also is Cartecay, which means "bread valley," a beautiful area of Gilmer County where many apples are grown today. And if one ever has seen the breathtaking 729-foot Amicalola Falls in Dawson County, it is easy to understand that "Amicalola" means "tumbling water."

There are some cases in which the Indian words have deviated from their original meanings. For example, "Etowah" has an obscure origin. A possible Cherokee word is "etawaha" or "deadwood." A similar Creek word is "Italwa," meaning "town." There are many places in North Georgia with this name. In fact, "Hightower," is a corruption of the pronunciation. (Towns County has an Upper Hightower and a Lower Hightower.) And, of course, there was an ancient Indian tribe and a settlement both named Etowah; the settlement was located near Cartersville.

One of the most interesting misinterpretations of a word is "Untsai 'yi," which translated means "brass." This is why the valley in which I was born and reared was called Brasstown Valley and the highest mountain in Georgia, at 4,784 feet, is Brasstown Bald. Actually, the correct Indian word was "Itse 'yi," or "green valley," and anyone who has driven from Hiawassee to Young Harris and looked down into one of the most beautiful valleys in the world would have no trouble with the correct translation.

Some Indian word corruptions have taken unusual turns. For example, there is a mountain in Habersham County called Sillycook Mountain. It is a corruption of "saligugi," which means "turtle."

Some picturesque names were given by the white man. The early settlers thought the mountains when seen from a distance had a blue appearance and called them the Blue Ridge Mountains. They saw someone going barefooted and named this isolated little settlement "Barefoot" in the corner of Towns County. It, by the way, was where a young college student ran off with a local girl and got married in the early 1900's. His name was E. D. Rivers, who later became Governor of Georgia.

Many mountain customs and beliefs are as quaint and picturesque as are mountain names. Nowhere is there to be found more mountain ingenuity than in the many home remedies for various ailments. They probably developed because there always was a scarcity of medical doctors in the mountains, and, too, mountaineers usually are suspicious of medical treatment and fearful of hospitals.

My father was sick for a long time before he finally was persuaded he needed professional medical attention. By then, it was too late. To this day, my mother is very negative about doctors and hospitals, and, although some of my best friends are medical doctors, I must confess that I share that fear and will postpone seeing the doctor. I think it must have something to do with a subconscious fear that they may find something wrong with us.

At any rate, the lack of medical facilities or lack of personal gumption resulted in the development of many remedies handed down from generation to generation just as dialect and political affiliations have been.

In my discussion here I have not tried to make any detailed list but will mention only a few of the most common of which I have heard all my life.

Household items and natural products often were used for medicinal purposes. Things like turpentine, kerosene, oil, flour, soot, lard, sugar, salt, whiskey, honey, onions and potatoes were common ingredients of mountain prescriptions and treatments.

A mixture of lard and chimney soot was used to stop bleeding. Lard and flour were used for burns as was salty water. Another remedy was to place small pieces of raw potato on the burned spots. Salt fat pork was used to "draw" boils and infections to a head for lancing.

Broken bones seldom were put in casts. I had three broken arms as a boy—once when I fell from a tree, again when I tripped over a tree root and, finally, when I wrecked a bicycle. Only when I had a really bad break while we were in Atlanta did Birdie take me to the hospital and have a cast put on it. Birdie fell down the basement steps a few years ago, and, only by great persuasion bordering on force, did Hoyle get her to go to the hospital to have an obviously broken arm set. Before two weeks passed, she had taken a knife and removed the plaster cast.

No ailments brought forth as many different concoctions as did colds and the "croup." Poultices of fried onions applied with an outing cloth were common. Some used wool soaked in kerosene, turpentine and/or lard. Although doctors say there is no cure for the common cold, mountaineers "cured" colds with several remedies: a tablespoon of whiskey and onions, a tablespoon of burned whiskey, a mixture of vinegar and honey, tea made of pine needles or red pepper or sauerkraut juice.

Asthma was a common malady which could be relieved by inhaling salty water through the nose and cured by keeping a Chihuahua dog around the house. Carrying a buckeye would ward off rheumatism, and to insure against ever having a headache, one would put clippings of his hair under a rock.

I frequently had the earache as a youngster, and this was one illness which frightened my mother inasmuch as my father's fatal illness had started with one. Numerous remedies were tried, such as holding my head close to the fire or a lamp, or putting drops of castor oil or small solutions of salty water in my ear. Many other remedies were proposed which Birdie turned down. I remember one well-meaning neighbor advocating "bug juice." and other mothers suggesting machine oil and a few drops of urine.

"Baby mouth" or "thrash" was a common ailment when I was young. It was an infection of the mouth or throat of a nursing infant. Mrs. Callie Nichols, the lady who had held me while Birdie gathered the rocks from the creek, had a community-wide reputation of being able to cure this by breathing into the infant's mouth

There were other remedies for this common condition. One was to give the baby a drink of spring water out of a stranger's hat. Another was to pass the baby backwards through a white mule's collar. Still another was to stick a duck's bill in the baby's mouth. An old, old remedy for a "fretful" child was catnip tea.

Nearly every mountain child was stung frequently by bees or "pack saddlers" and was given relief by ointments made of tobacco juice or snuff. Many times I've been covered from head to toe with "chiggers" or poison ivy. "Chiggers" could be killed by putting nail polish on each bite, or a butter-and-salt application would help. For poison ivy, baking soda and water, green tomato juice or buttermilk was used to relieve the itching.

Nothing brought out as many recommendations for home remedies as getting rid of warts which, naturally, everyone knew were the result of playing with toad frogs. A few I remember included tying a hair from the tail of a horse around the wart, putting blood from the wart on a grain of corn and feeding it to a chicken, wiping a stolen dishrag on the warts and putting a small stone in a paper bag and putting the bag in a fork in the road. Another big remedy was to stick the hand with the wart in the bag, tie the bag (with hand removed, of course), and leave it in the road so that the person who comes along and opens the bag will get the wart. Some old-timers claimed they could "charm" the wart away by rubbing it and saying a few secret words.

As playing with frogs was certain to give one warts, so

playing in mud holes would give one worms. The cure for worms was eating lots of poke sallet. I never worried about having worms, but I would not eat the rhubarb which supposedly would keep me healthy.

Not only do mountaineers believe in their remedies handed down from generation to generation but also they believe in doing things "by the signs." Again, the list could run on and on, especially as it relates to the moon.

Homemade soap will not set if it is not made in the full of the moon. Shingles will curl if split or nailed down while the moon is growing, and the ideal time to put them down is when the points of the moon are turned down. Fence posts must be set in the old of the moon when its size is decreasing or they will loosen. This also is the time that crops must be harvested or they will rot and not keep well.

The opposite is true for killing hogs. This must be done when the moon's size is increasing or the bacon from that hog will shrink when it is fried. The ideal time to set hens is three weeks before the full of the moon. A circle around the moon means rain, and it is bad luck to see a new moon for the first time through the trees.

In addition to the moon, mountaineers observe nature around them for signs of importance. Some would call such beliefs superstitions, and well they may be, but the question remains that, if they haven't worked with some regularity, why have they endured?

One of the oldest I remember is that one can tell what kind of general weather the year will bring by observing the first 12 days of the year. For example, if it snows on January 1st, most of the month will be snowy; if it rains on the third day, March generally will be rainy.

Actions of birds and animals also are significant in the mountains.

Nearly everyone has heard of Ground Hog Day, February 2nd, when, if the animal sees his shadow, he returns to his burrow and winter will last another six weeks. Old-timers have a variation on this. They say the real Ground Hog Day is February 14th and the resulting winter is 40 days, not six weeks. Shirley's father was an avid ground hog or "whistle pig" hunter and he always has said that, if he caught one that was fat or had darker and heavier fur, it was going to be a cold winter.

Blue Jays were considered signs of bad luck. I always heard that these noisy, mean-tempered birds were owned by the devil and "That's why they are so full of devilment." When one was seen with a stick or a straw in its mouth, which was often, it was said to be carrying it to hell.

Another animal read for signs was the house cat. If it lay with its back to the fire, the weather was certain to turn cold.

Fire also could tell one certain things about the weather as well as family relations. If the fire "tramps" or makes a soft, sputtering sound, snow could be expected very soon. If the fire burns brightly and leaps up into the chimney, there is going to be a family fuss in the near future.

Heavy corn shucks, thick bark on trees and tough apple skins also mean a cold winter. Very few insects in the summer are a sure sign that a cold winter is coming.

Perhaps some of these things seem strange, but one must remember that mountain people were tied closely to the land and the weather.

There are many other little superstitions. Daisies are picked and the petals pulled one by one to count off "she loves me, she loves me not," until the last petal tells what one's girlfriend thinks of him. Dandelion thistles sent flying with a puff of breath make wishes come true, with the number of thistles remaining on the stem representing the number of years before the wish will be realized.

Hours were spent hunting four-leaf clovers for good luck and, when one was found, it was pressed in the dictionary or the Bible or placed in one's left shoe to assure meeting the person one is going to marry.

An itching nose is a sure sign that company is coming.

Unless one kisses the hem of a turned-up dress, she will become an old maid. One should not trade anything if a bird flies up at his feet, and a baby shown his image in a mirror will grow up to be two-faced.

If one drops an eating utensil when setting a table, company is coming. "Knife falls, man calls; fork falls, woman calls; spoon falls, child calls."

One of the biggest disappointments I can remember occurred when I discovered that it does not rain little frogs. After a hard summer rain there usually would be hundreds of frogs no bigger than a thumbnail all over the dirt roads that ran beside our home. As a little fellow, I was told that it had rained them and the worms that seemed to be plentiful. I later learned that they came from tadpoles, and, as a boy, I gathered Mason fruit jars full of slimy strings of frog eggs, kept them until they turned into tadpoles and, subsequently, little frogs, a process almost as miraculous as raining frogs.

The strength and importance of custom in the lives of men have been the subject of observations and writings from the beginning of recorded history. It was Ovid who said, "Nothing is stronger than custom," and Plutarch who wrote, "Custom is almost a second nature." Edmund Burke summed it up with the observation that "custom reconciles us to everything."

Never were these sayings truer than in the mountains of North Georgia.

XI

# My Music

*The setting sun, and music at the close*
*As the last taste of sweets is sweetest last,*
*Writ in remembrance, more than things long past.*

*King Richard II*
William Shakespeare

I can see the scene as clearly as if it were yesterday. Our radio sat on a black wooden table in the corner of the living room. It was a Silvertone from Sears and Roebuck with a round, greenish dial and four knobs. From that magic box came many wondrous sounds but none that touched me more deeply nor endured so long as the ones I got by turning the dial to 650 on Saturday nights.

Jack Nichols, a friend who died a very young man, had introduced me to the Grand Ole Opry when I was at his home one Saturday night. WSM Radio was a 50,000-watt clear channel station and was one of the few stations one could get in the mountains at night. Even then there was great difficulty. I remember pouring water on the ground to make the station come in clearer and, another time, holding the ground wire in my hand.

From that night more than 35 years ago, when I heard

142

the magic of Bill Monroe, Roy Acuff and others, until now I have been addicted to country music. Seldom does a day go by that I don't listen to an hour or so of it, usually while I am riding somewhere. I know where all the country music stations are located and have hundreds of record albums. I traveled alone in the early phase of my campaign, and for several months country music on the radio was my only companion. A person who travels with me had better like country music because he will hear plenty of it. Pat Jarvis and Gene Brown both met that qualification.

Of course, country music has changed over the years, and today it is different things to different people. There is the country-rock of Kristoffersen, Waylon Jennings and Willie Nelson, the Cajun of Doug Kershaw, the honkytonk of George Jones, the Bluegrass of Bill Monroe, etc.

All of these have the same roots in the culture and tradition of the mountains of Appalachia. That is where its soul originated and lives. These hard-living people had hard-living songs.

Its originators, like the Carter Family and Chet Atkins, came out of these hills, and innovators like Earl Scruggs and Dolly Parton also were born and reared there.

Ronnie Milsap, a former student of mine at Young Harris College and one of the newest Nashville superstars, also is from this mountain area.

One wonders why so much music tradition has come from this relatively small geographical area. Again, it is something that goes back to the music the mountain pioneers brought with them and handed down from generation to generation.

The Scotch-Irish settlers brought their music with them from the British Isles to New England, the Virginia and Carolina Tidelands and on over into the mountains.

Fiddles were easy to carry and the early settlers brought these instruments with them. This instrument is called the violin in other segments of the music field, and people assume that since the violin is used by symphonies that "violin" is the older term. However, "fiddle" has been used much longer. A Chaucer poem of 1205 refers to a fiddle. For most of our country music's history it has been the dominant instrument. Up until the 1920's, it was the lead instrument in most bands, with different regions having different fiddle styles. The North Georgia sound and the Cajun and Western sounds are vastly different.

The beginning of the country music industry as we know it today dates from June, 1923, when Fiddlin' John Carson, who was born and reared in Blue Ridge in mountainous Fannin County, recorded two songs for Okeh Records in Atlanta. They were "The Little Old Log Cabin in the Lane" and "The Old Hen Cackled and the Rooster's Going to Crow." Radio station WSB played these and was one of the pioneer stations in promoting this music. Later Fiddlin' John was to go to New York and record "You Will Never Miss Your Mother Until She Is Gone" and "Pop's Billy Goat." Carson played at Tom Watson's and later at Eugene Talmadge's political rallies with his daughter, Moonshine Kate.

The guitar also found its way into the mountains, although it was considered a woman's instrument. There are many different kinds of playing styles, depending upon the fingers used, their placement on the strings and whether a pick is used. Mother Maybelle Carter is the artist who usually is credited with the innovations which have made the guitar the lead instrument since the 1930's. Of course, later Chet Atkins, who got his start with the Carter Family, was to influence the entire music industry with his unique style.

The banjo came along during the middle 1800's when the minstrel show was popular. The early banjos had four strings and, in a way, were a cross between a drum and a stringed instrument. The head is a round hoop with a stretched skin, or drumhead. It was played with a style called "frailing" or "clawhammer." Uncle Dave Macon, who generally is regarded as the first Grand Ole Opry star, played the banjo. Mountain men liked the instrument and tuned it to play in a lonesome-sounding mode.

When a 19-year old mountain boy named Earl Scruggs joined Bill Monroe in 1945, he brought a revolutionary way of playing which changed banjo-picking completely, and some will say this really was the beginning of Bluegrass music. It was a style he had developed himself, using a three-finger technique on the five strings that had a driving sound and syncopated style.

The mountain music tradition also has something to do with the fact that, in the isolated coves and valleys shut off from the outside world, one had little else to do after the sun had gone down and the chores were finished except to sit around with a musical instrument. Nothing can fill hours of loneliness nor overcome the drudgery of the day as well as music.

More of these people could play an instrument, it seems, than could not play. And in some families every single member, from the oldest to the youngest, male and female, could play a fiddle, guitar, "banjer," mandolin, mouth harp, autoharp or some other instrument. Many could play more than one instrument, and some made their instruments or improvised. Playing spoons or a saw was common, and I know one man who plays a hubcap.

In fact, people devised new homemade instruments which created new sounds such as Bluegrass. The zither, a many-stringed instrument which has musical tones much like those of a harp, was popular. One instrument believed to have been created in the mountains was the dulcimer, which is similar to the zither but usually has only three or four strings. A turkey quill usually was used to strum the strings, and some also used a small stick called a "noter." It combines the tone of a wooden instrument with the tune of bagpipes.

An old-time fiddler, Lee Kirby, was a great friend, and I spent many enjoyable hours sitting on his front porch and leaning against a post while Lee would sit in a chair bottomed with pieces of a rubber innertube and go from one fiddle tune to another. He would sing lyrics of some but he played only the melody of others. After a "ditty," as he called short, fast numbers, he would cock his head to one side and inquire, "Did that one pleasure you?" He might then follow with a mournful, wailing song and then with a stomp of his feet do a "play-game" piece. That would be a tune like "Froggie Went A-Courtin' " or "Skip to My Lou."

Lee could not remember the names to some, and he never knew the titles of others. But his repertoire was unbelievable. Some I've heard from other musicians in different versions. The famous "Frankie and Johnny" is from a mountain song called "Frankie Baker."

The harmonies were often monotonous, but this was the desired effect. "Darlin'," for example, could go on for as long as one's imagination could carry it:

"Oh, darlin', you can't love but one
 You can't love but one and have any fun.
 You can't love three and still be true to me.
 You can't love four and love me anymore . . ."

And so on, ad infinitum.

One of my favorites was "Wildwood Flower" played on a guitar, and another was the mournful "Down in the Valley," especially the first verse, "If you don't love me, love whom you please, but throw your arms around me, give my heart ease." Or "The Big-Eyed Rabbit," which goes: "The rabbit's the kind of thing that travels in the dark, it never knows when danger's 'round 'till he hears old Rover bark." This sounds like a novelty tune or one of those "without no harm in them," as Lee would say. Really, it's about some man stealing the singer's wife.

Of course, old hymns were sung and played. One I can recall was "The Hallelujah Christian," which I've never heard anywhere else.

I loved the old hymns and mentioned them in a previous chapter about going to the Baptist Church during revival week. I also went in the summer to what was known as "singin' school" where a singing master would lead off on a tune, and the rest of us would "jine in."

Shirley grew up in the same environment. She remembers going down to "the mouth of the cove" where she lived and stringing beans or shelling peas in the summer while Roe Young played one of his home-made fiddles and his sister, "Mame," played an old pump organ which she pedaled for dear life to keep the air flowing.

Country music artists are really poets, much the same as Byron Herbert Reece was a poet, or as the wandering minstrels of centuries ago played for the common folk while the king's scop reported only to the castle personnel.

Over a century ago many mountain communities had balladeers who, through their songs, carried the news of the time. This tradition was carried over by Bascomb Lamar Lunsford, known as the Minstrel of the Appalachians. A native of Mars Hill, North Carolina, this great folklorist was asked to record some of his songs for the Columbia University Library in the 1930's. He complied by singing 375 of them.

The country music singers have been able to reach a far larger audience than most modern-day poets.

Bill Anderson, one of the greatest of all the contemporary songwriters, is a graduate of the University of Georgia School of Journalism. His grandfather was a District Superintendent in the Methodist Church and preached thousands of sermons to the mountaineers and others in his lifetime.

Before he died he talked with his famous grandson from his deathbed. "Bill," he said, "I don't know much about this business you're in, but I do know this: That one of your songs will be heard by more people than have heard all of my sermons combined."

In my opinion, one of the greatest sermons I've ever heard is a three-minute song of Bill's, "I Can Do Nothing Alone."

Bill, who grew up in DeKalb County, Georgia, is a good friend whose talent I respect. Since he went to

Nashville, Tennessee, from Commerce, Georgia, where he had been a disc jockey and had written "City Lights" from the top of the local three-story hotel, Bill has become one of country music's most consistent songwriters. There hardly has been a time in fifteen years that he has not had one of his songs on the charts.

Each October for many years I have gone to Nashville for the annual Disc Jockey Convention. Each record company has shows with its artists performing, and one can listen to country music almost around-the-clock for one solid week. The first trip I made was with Billy Dilworth, a long-time friend.

I could not discuss country music without mentioning Billy Dilworth. Already immortalized in Paul Hemphill's excellent work on country music, anything I might add would be superfluous. He is the close friend who prompted my study of the history of country music. Before meeting Billy, I knew I liked what I heard, but I did not know the history of the artists nor how they came to write certain songs.

Not only is Billy an award-winning reporter, but each Saturday for fifteen years he also has emceed a country music show on Radio Station WLET in Toccoa, Georgia.

It is one of the most-listened-to radio shows in all of North Georgia. I've spent many pleasant Saturdays listening to Billy spin records and chat with anyone calling in. It also has been fun to sit in on the program which, like the Grand Ole Opry, is mass confusion in the studio but, somehow, comes out great on the airwaves.

Many country music records are being made by Georgians. Few states have produced more bona fide country music artists. A partial list includes Mac Davis, Stonewall Jackson, Roy Drusky, Brenda Lee, LaWanda Lindsey, Ray Stevens, Jerry Reed, Joe South, Freddie Weller, Pete Drake, David Rodgers and the already-mentioned Bill Anderson. Gospel music, one of the roots of this kind of music, has these native Georgians: The Lewis

Family, Wendell Bagwell, Martha Carson, Hovie Lister and the LeFevres.

Country humor always has been an important part of the country music heritage as exemplified by Junior Samples on the popular television program "Hee-Haw." This Georgian was "discovered" when he gave a Department of Natural Resources Public Information man a tall tale about a fish he supposedly had caught on Lake Lanier.

Two members of the Country Music Hall of Fame also lived in Georgia. Uncle Art Satherly spent many years in Savannah, and Minnie Pearl lived five years in Newnan.

As a teenager and later as a young man, I spent most Friday and Saturday nights at square dances. They usually were held at a high school gym and, for a number of years, at a place known as Club Nottley. A band consisting of a fiddler, a banjo picker, a guitar player and sometimes a piano player would play old tunes like "Bile 'Em Cabbage Down," "Soldier's Joy" and "Down Yonder." To this day, I can't keep my feet still when I hear one of these old tunes.

I learned early to call square dances and usually would be admitted free to perform this service. The mountain square dance started with a big circle and is unlike the modern square dancing done by the square dance teams of today. From the circle, you would "couple up four" and do all kinds of gyrations and designs such as "put the birdie in the cage," then "birdie out, the hoot owl in, the hoot owl out and gone again." Or, "four hands up, four hands over, first couple form that four-leaf clover." Most would end by swinging the "corner lady" and then "your own sweet honey baby." Sometimes we would break off on a "shoo-fly swing."

We would do what we called "smooth dancing," but some would mix in "clogging" or "clog dancing." The "clog" is the old-fashioned mountain dancing which, like the early music, was brought over by our forefathers. I read somewhere that Henry VIII once took Ann Boleyn onto the dance floor with the remark, "Let the music knock it." Anyone who has observed clogging would know exactly what the old king meant. It is similar to the Irish jig, and the music comes from the jigs and reels of England and Scotland.

Very few youngsters grow up in the mountains without learning how to clog. In Towns County alone there must be a dozen clogging groups, from toddlers to older persons, that get together weekly to clog. Some travel throughout the Southeast giving performances and demonstrations. An entire day at the Georgia Mountain Fair in Hiawassee is filled with clogging groups, and on a weekend in May and another in October clogging festivals are held in Hiawassee.

Most of the music I heard as a boy around Young Harris is what now is called Bluegrass. This is another name for traditional country, or "ole timey" music, as some called it, although some purists will argue that "ole timey" music is different and that Bluegrass is a relatively new sound. Certainly it has enjoyed a recent revival, and its popularity extends to college campuses and giant festivals held all over the country.

Basically, it was unamplified music, and the fiddle, mandolin or banjo handled the lead instead of the guitar. It got the name from Bill Monroe's Bluegrass Boys who came out of Kentucky to make this kind of music popular in the 1930's and 1940's. Later, Lester Flatt and Earl Scruggs continued the tradition in the 1950's and on until the present.

One of my favorite instruments always has been the autoharp. Some claim it is the oldest of the stringed instruments, and few musicians use it today. "Pop" Stoneman and Mother Maybelle Carter were highly skilled with it, and some of my fondest memories are hearing the "Black Mountain Rag" played by these artists.

"Pop" held his on his lap when he played it; Mother Maybelle held hers up high on her chest. The autoharp consists of about 50 metal strings stretched across a frame over a sound box. Pressing on a buttom for a particular chord bar controls the strings so that moving a pick across them produces the desired sound.

One artist whose roots are deep in our area is Hedy West whose father came from Union County and whose uncle, Harold, published the *North Georgia News* in Blairsville and *The Towns County Herald.* As a teenager, Hedy attracted national attention performing in folk festivals. She worked with Pete Seeger at the Village Gate in New York City and performed widely in Europe. In 1963, she joined with Bobby Bare to write "500 Miles Away from Home."

Speaking of Bare, probably no song ever has captured as well the longing of mountain boys, displaced, homesick and working in the North as "Detroit City," which has the line, "By day I make the cars, by night I make the bars." How many friends I had who left the mountains to do just that!

One cannot discuss country music without mentioning the legendary Hank Williams. Like the itinerant minstrels of old, Hank traveled the tank towns and played the schoolhouses in the 1940's before making it big on the Grand Ole Opry in 1949. Like a meteor flashing across the sky, he burned briefly and then died in 1953 at the age of 29. However, he left some 100 songs that continue to be popular not only in country music but in the pop field as well.

During the height of his popularity, I listened every night to WCKY, a radio station in Cincinnati, Ohio. It was a station that began playing country music each night at ten o'clock, and many, many nights I have stayed up to hear Hank and Lefty Frizell, Webb Pierce and Kitty Wells.

I think one reason country music is so popular is that it speaks for those too inhibited to express their emotions. I've heard it referred to as "music which articulates the feeling of the inarticulate." That is a little condescending. I've known dozens of musicians who are too shy to tell you how they feel, but put an instrument in their hands and their sensitivity comes through very expressively. Many well-known artists are like that today. Mell Tillis is an example of one who stutters when he talks but has written some excellent songs and is a great singer and comedian.

As in baseball with Hoyle Bryson and literature with "Hub" Reece, there were musicians in the mountains who could have made names for themselves professionally if they could have brought themselves to leave their beloved mountains.

Fiddlin' Howard Cunningham of Hiawassee is one of these. The Master of Ceremonies at all the music programs of the Georgia Mountain Fair, Howard has been a premier fiddler for years. Largely by his efforts Hiawassee has become known as the country music capital of Georgia, and many fans prefer the authenticity of Howard, Banjoist Don Fox, and Jim "Chief" Childers to the Nashville celebrities.

Until a person attends one of these mountain music festivals in Hiawassee, he has missed some of the best and most authentic music being played anywhere today. It also has done a great deal for the pride of these shy mountain musicians who have discovered that they must be pretty good for people to come so many miles to hear them.

There still are country songs about slipping around, drinking, trucks and human failings and woes, but today many also comment on such contemporary subjects as ecology and harmonious relationships between races.

Persons who previously had looked down on country music are accepting it. Its fans are coming out of the closet. Author Kurt Vonnegut, Jr., is a fan. The astronauts played Conway Twitty's "Hello, Darling" to the Russian cosmonauts. Loretta Lynn appeared on the cover of *Newsweek* and Merle Haggard on *Time.* One-fifth of all the records sold in the United States today are country songs. Fifteen years ago there were 80 country music radio stations in the United States; today they number 1,000!

Why the appeal? Bill Anderson, who has given much

thought to it, answered *Augusta Herald* reporter Don Rhodes this way: "Country music is primarily a lyrical music. It tells a story of love or of sadness, of hope or frustration, of God, of mother and home . . . just a story about life and its parade. As a songwriter the greatest compliment I can receive is for someone to say to me, 'You must have written that song just for me because that's just the way I feel.' "

A *New York Times* reporter, Christopher Wren, is quoted in the *Country Music Encyclopedia* (Melvin Shestok, Crowell & Co., 1974) with this definition: "Country music is really a story, told plain, of people trying to get along the best they can. It is music from the ground up where the lyrics override the melody . . . country music is traditionally rural southern in its origin, conservative in its politics (but with a stubborn streak of gut liberalism), blue collar in its economics, blatantly patriotic, fundamentalist about God, and nostalgic about Jesus. It distrusts urban wealth and intellect . . ."

Yes, that's my music.

# XII

# The Mountains Today

*I am homesick for the mountains—*
*My heroic mother hills—*
*And the longing that is on me*
*No solace ever stills.*

Anonymous

Tremendous changes have been wrought in the Georgia Mountains during the past quarter century, particularly the last decade. Many of them have been good and have resulted in progress and prosperity beyond the wildest dreams of all but the youngest descendants of the hardy pioneers whose struggles fashioned the unique civilization that has been the subject and inspiration of this book. Some, unfortunately, have raised questions of the future of the splendid geography and admirable culture of this cradle of unspoiled nature and independent man.

The rugged ridges and isolated valleys which for centuries served as buffers against the encroachments of the outside world now function as beacons for an ever-growing invasion of the region by those who seek respite from the grime and pressures of industrial proliferation and metropolitan sophistication. By the tens of thousands they come each year to see the sights and enjoy the pleasures of mountain existence, and many return to make their homes. They bring with them the dollars of affluence which are welcome and needed, but some of them also bring with them habits of unconcern for the maintenance of the delicate nature they come to enjoy—habits that are most unwelcome and distressing. It has been said that Americans cannot enjoy anything without spoiling it, and it is a source of concern to natives like me that such not happen to our beloved mountains.

Happily, most of the development which has taken place to date has been done by men and women of vision who understand this and have sought to accommodate change and growth without jeopardizing beauty and values. The exploiters and fast-buck artists have been discouraged and speculation minimized on an individual basis, but more and more thoughtful leaders are coming to the realization that ultimately some statutory direction must be given from the state level to assure that future development is orderly and substantial and that the ecology of the mountains is maintained not only for the present but also for generations to come. Zoning and planning are anathema to the independent mountain spirit, but love of the mountains and the desire to protect them are even stronger sentiments which, I believe, in the not-too-distant future will prevail in the form of laws which will give state guidance and assistance to local governments in planning and directing growth and development for progress and prosperity in keeping with local wishes while protecting and preserving nature's balance and beauty.

Thinking back to my childhood, I often wonder how some of the old-timers who viewed "furriners" and their ways with such great suspicion and apprehension would react to the influx of outsiders today. They probably would "spin in their graves" if they saw the thousands of tourist cars zipping around the mountains of which the crossing, in their days, was an ordeal indeed. I remember hearing at the "loafers' bench" about how difficult it was to cross Unicoi Gap in a Model-T Ford and how the owner of one would have to stop at the crest, cut down a stout sapling and tie it behind the car as a brake in order to be able to descend at a safe speed. Today's automobiles do it without shifting gears, although the foolhardy and unwary can overheat their power brakes in a hurry if they try to descend too fast.

Ingress and egress continue to be matters of controversy in the Georgia mountains, but in a different way. The debate today is about building new superhighways to get more cars in and out faster. And, while the convenience and speed of multi-lane highways are appealing from the standpoints of time and convenience, the idea of scarring the virgin landscape of the untouched peaks and valleys with four-lane concrete and asphalt ribbons is repugnant not only to ecologists but also to mountain purists like me. The State Transportation Department has recognized this strong feeling on the part of many with its decision to terminate the controversial Georgia Highway 400 Project at Dahlonega and to go around the heart of the Georgia mountains with a western by-pass along the present roadbed of Highway 5 to its junction with Highway 76. To have done otherwise would have been a desecration of the last unspoiled mountain wilderness in Georgia and, although the proposed straight-line route would have benefited me in cutting off an hour of driving time from Atlanta to Young Harris, I much prefer to take an extra hour and have the mountains preserved intact.

Another recurring issue is the proposed extension of the Blue Ridge Parkway from North Carolina into Georgia. The same convincing arguments which prevailed against Highway 400 apply to this, and I have been pleased that federal authorities to date have resisted efforts to proceed with this extension. As delightful as it might be to have such a scenic drive and as beneficial as it might be to the tourists we want to attract into North Georgia, the damage which would be done to the mountains by building it would be greater than any of the advantages which might be achieved.

The purpose of going to the mountains is to relax and enjoy their scenery and delights, and it is defeated by funneling high-speed traffic through them on ugly superhighways. Existing routes should be improved and, where possible, made three lanes on the upgrades, but building new superhighways over untouched ridges seems to me to be a profaning of our responsibility to preserve a unique and wonderful region of our State for the benefit and enjoyment of citizens today and generations to come.

The ideal kind of development and of tourist attraction for North Georgia is epitomized by the Georgia Mountain Fair held for nine days each year in August under the sponsorship of the Towns County Lions Club in the quaint and colorful mountain town of Hiawassee, a sister community to Young Harris, where I grew up. It is all a fair should be and more, because it is an exposition of mountain culture and crafts totally devoid of commercial exploitation, and all of its proceeds over costs go into needed community projects and worthy statewide causes like the Lighthouse for the Blind. It has grown in 25 years from a small exhibition of mountain crafts into a major national event which yearly attracts more than 150,000 visitors. For many years I served on its Board of Directors.

The father of the mountain fair is a man who is as colorful and as representative of the North Georgia Mountains as are its exhibits—Herbert Tabor, of Ellijay, who is known as "Tall Tabor" throughout the area where his name and that of insurance are synonymous. The son of a long-time political leader and Ordinary of Gilmer County, "Tall Tabor" is another of Young Harris College's distinguished alumni who started off as a banker and then opened the first insurance business in the mountains.

Atlanta *Constitution* Columnist Celestine Sibley wrote about him back in 1954, and no one could improve on her description of him as follows:

"The way he conducts his personal business is unique

everywhere but in the mountains and is probably a system fast disappearing in that land of lakes and indigo peaks. If anybody wishes to buy his insurance they flag him down on his way to round up exhibits for the fair or take a sick neighbor to the doctor. Sometimes they have to follow him to the hills where he goes in search of an especially fine winter apple, a jar of sourwood honey or some cracklings. If they're lucky they can catch him at the loafer's bench in front of the courthouse after supper on a summer evening or sitting in front of the general store in Young Harris, chatting with his old friend Professor Adams, on Wednesday nights.

"The mountains are his main business. He loves them. He loves mountain people and knows hundreds of stories about them. He never misses a mountain event if he can help it, be it a cemetery working or a Young Harris vesper service on top of Brasstown Bald. Any business that interfered with his pleasure in his country and his active participation in its growth would not be worth his time, I know.

"Herbert Tabor has to leave the mountains sometimes. The common good occasionally brings him to Atlanta and he has been known to travel to other states but he considers that a waste of time. His eyes twinkle when he refers to the mountain country as the U.S.A., but he means it."

The idea for the Mountain Fair came to "Tall Tabor" back in 1950 when, as a non-resident member of the Towns County Lions Club who traveled across the mountains from Ellijay every Wednesday to attend, he became intrigued by the continuing discussion of his fellow Club Members and town leaders about what the Town of Hiawassee could do about its "nothing future" and dwindling population. In his words:

"I figured we might as well be doing something useful, so I suggested at one meeting that we organize a fair. The club got behind it and look what happened."

While the Club and the townspeople went to work

with vigor, few really expected the acceptance and interest which resulted. Although the first fair in 1950 was little more than a few crude exhibits of mountain products and crafts, more than 1,000 people from Towns and surrounding counties attended. That was enough to convince the Club that it was on to a good thing and, in 1951, with "Tall Tabor" serving as General Chairman, the members decided to hold a "whole-week" affair. Chairman Tabor sat down and in his own inimitable style wrote an open letter which was circulated to every house in Towns and surrounding counties and now is a collector's item. Dated June 14, 1951, it reads:

"Dear Friend:

"The first whole-week Fair in our area will be held as per this letterhead, complete with a 20-unit carnival, and an auction sale of curio-antiques, which we believe will be something new.

"We are inviting and urging you, and a number of other outstanding people, who, like us, are interested in the development of our section, to help create public interest, encourage exhibits, and help in every other possible way to make the Fair a success, and a credit to our counties. It will have to be good!

"In addition to the usual features of a fair, we plan an auto show of every 1951 make and model, plus a few aged specimens, a one-day flower show, a one-day livestock show, an all-week poultry show, the auction sale similar to the car sales where an item is offered but may be withdrawn unless it brings a set minimum price or more, and a speech by Governor Herman Talmadge. Our mountains are full of old and odd things of little or no value to their owners, but which might bring fancy prices at the sale, which will be widely advertised.

"The first name on each list attached is a club member, and he, the County and Home Demonstration Agents, the Mountain Experiment Station, or this office will be happy to furnish information, suggestions and cooperation on anything you want to do about the Fair, which is intended to show ourselves and all visitors what we have in these mountains, and to attract settlers and more visitors for the benefit of all concerned.

"The Premium List booklet will be mailed to you when received from the printers about August 1st, but work on exhibits should be started now, especially on livestock, flowers and crop items.

"We are counting on you.

"Cordially yours,

"/s/H. Tabor

"General Chairman."

The success of the Mountain Fair from that point was taken up by the *Mountain News* of Hiawassee in a front page article published in 1975 as follows:

"The Lions' decision to have a non-commercial fair on a regional basis was the key to eventual success. Twenty-five years later the basic idea hasn't changed. There are no commercial exhibits. Few items are sold, and those that are are handmade and native to the area. The midway, a strictly family one, has been operated by 'Honest Homer' Scott for the last nineteen years. Even the annual parade displays no commercialism. It's restricted to antique cars and horse-drawn vehicles with entries coming from miles around.

"While the Fair was Tabor's idea, the idea of preserving examples of the ancient mountain way of life in Pioneer Village was suggested by Lion E.N. Nicholson. It was he and his wife who promoted the growing event for the first ten years. As unpaid managers, they rounded up exhibits and persuaded people to volunteer their services for the activity.

"In 1961 the Nicholsons retired and Towns County Lion Bob Anderson, the current Fair President, assumed the helm. Mr. Anderson is to be commended for the sacrificial giving of his time, without pay, for so many years to the Fair which continues to be a success.

"During the years the Fair's impact has been increasingly greater upon the mountain area. Like a huge stone tossed into the economic lake, the ripples are spreading farther and farther. Motels within a 75-mile radius know when the nine-day event is underway. Space becomes scarce and reservations are necessary. Local businessmen directly feel the impact. They can't avoid it when 100,000 visitors pour into the little community."

The continuing economic impact of the Mountain Fair was reported in an article in *Family Weekly* on August 16, 1970, in these words:

"When the Fair started, 20 years ago, Hiawassee had no visitors and perhaps only two dozen summer homes. Today it has nearly 400 summer residences. Its two supermarkets together gross over a million dollars a year. Its bank deposits nearly doubled during the month of August when the fair was held. Clearly, by using their heads and a once taken-for-granted asset, the good people of Hiawassee have rescued their town from the brink of its economic grave."

The Sunday *Atlanta Journal-Constitution* in a Dixie Living Section feature on August 1, 1971, headed by a full-cover photograph of the authentic copper moonshine still which is the top attraction of the Fair (which had my old friend "Thee" King in the foreground simulating a drink from a jug of mountain moonshine), recounted what it is like attending the Mountain Fair:

"So popular is the homespun fair that many attend year after year, being sure of accommodations by reserving rooms a year in advance. Others come with camping gear and in recreational vehicles, taking advantage of the Lions Club campgrounds nearby on the shore of Lake Chatuge. The impact of the fair is felt in motels as far away as Interstate 85.

"The nine-day schedule is crowded with events ranging from appearances of nationally-known country music stars to a cloggers' convention; two gospel sings on Sundays; art and flower shows; livestock displays; an old-time, muzzle-loading, hog rifle shoot for a quarter of beef; and the annual mountain fair parade. And, of course, there's a midway featuring rides and various concessions.

"You can wander the free mountain-life exhibits and watch a board splitter making shingles with a froe, wood carvers turning chunks of wood into delicate figures and potters skillfully turning clay. You also can attend a quilting party, once a big social event in the life of mountaineers; visit an ancient mountain cabin, an old general store, and watch corn being ground into meal the old-fashioned way with a water-powered grist mill. Soap and hominy making are demonstrated as well as spinning and weaving. There's a collection of mountain farm implements which will baffle most of today's visitors.

"The Saturday parade, one of the highlights of the fair, is restricted to old cars and horsedrawn vehicles. There are ribbon awards for cooking competition and hobby exhibits. There is even a copper moonshine still."

The growing success of the Mountain Fair and the obvious conclusion that it had become a permanent and continuing event of the North Georgia scene convinced the Towns County Lions Club that it required a more permanent and adequate site than the campus of the Hiawassee High School. Accordingly, in keeping with its policy to use its profits to benefit the community and surrounding area, the Lions entered into an agreement with the Towns County Recreation Board to develop a combination recreation park and fair site. It made an initial contribution of $65,000 towards the development of the Towns County Recreation Park and, in cooperation with the Board, agreed to operate it on a year-round basis with activities to be scheduled every weekend including concerts, teen dances, country music shows, clogging, square dancing, blue grass music, gospel music, softball tournaments, camp-o-rees and water shows. Phase I of the 161-acre project was completed in March of 1976, including three ball fields and a new white-sand beach with adjoining bathhouse on Lake Chatuge. Phase II of the construction included the lighting and fencing of one ball field, paving of the parking lot for the beach and bath-house, expansion of the existing campground by 70 campsites, a comfort station and a multi-use amphitheater-type entertainment center. The official opening in con-junction with the 1976 fair marked an expenditure of ap-proximately $200,000, and long-range master plans for expansion over a five-year period call for more than 300 campsites, a pioneer village, tennis courts, nature trails, picnic areas with shelters, playgrounds, boat docks, a marina, an entertainment center and a community recrea-tion building.

In addition to all other activities, the Mountain Fair and its sponsoring Club also hold annual country music and cloggers festivals each fall and spring. Fiddlin' How-ard Cunningham has been the moving force in these events.

The people of Towns County have proved that prog-ress and prosperity can come hand-in-hand with the pres-ervation of culture, tradition and ecology. What they have accomplished is an example of channeling local resources, talents and ingenuity into meeting general public needs for recreation and vacation activities without sacrificing either local mores and traditions or the area's God-given assets of mother nature.

It is an example that already is being emulated in other areas of North Georgia, notably by the once-dying hamlet of Helen to the south, which has been transformed into an authentic replica of an Alpine Village and is attracting thousands of tourists with a year-round schedule of activi-ties which include an Oktoberfest, a Winter Festival, the annual Helen/Atlantic Balloon Race and the annual Chat-tahoochee River Championship Canoe and Kayak Races. It has a resident summer stock theater company which produces an imaginative version of Rodgers and Hammer-stein's classic musical "The Sound of Music." So success-ful has its experiment in planned tourist attraction been that the village is now planning to add 53 new buildings, including five new restaurants, a farmers market and a moat encircling the addition, at an estimated cost of $10 million.

Complementing Helen's attractions is the operation three miles away of the facilities and programs of the Unicoi Outdoor Recreation Station, including an impressive Lodge and Conference Center and comfortable cabin and camping facilities. The Station's facilities embrace those formerly known as Unicoi State Park and are adjacent to the Anna Ruby Falls Recreation Area administered by the U.S. Forest Service as part of the Chattahoochee National Forest.

This area represents a highly successful demonstration of the full utilization of natural, scenic and developed resources through the coordinated efforts of local, state, federal and private agencies and capital. It proves that intergovernmental cooperation and free enterprise development not only can co-exist but also complement each other for the benefit of all citizens as well as the economy of the region.

At the very edge of the North Georgia Mountains, an ambitious enterprise of the State Government has begun the realization of a tremendous potential through the development of the Lake Lanier Islands by the Lake Lanier Island Development Authority. This is a 1200-acre family recreation and resort area situated on a series of islands created by the impoundment of waters of the Chattahoochee River by Buford Dam. Lake Lanier already was one of the most often visited lakes in America, and with the addition of the state-sponsored-and-financed facilities developed by the Authority, it bodes to become one of the most popular and successful playgrounds in the Eastern United States. It includes an island for picnics, a white sand beach, bathhouse, golf course, rental houseboat fleet, rental sailboats, canoes, pontoons, catamarans and paddle boats, trout fishing ponds, riding stables, boat launching ramps, mini-golf, hotel, campground, cottages, restaurants, hiking trails, fishing of all kinds and even a cruise ship.

At the commercial and private-enterprise end of the spectrum, one has but to look to the northwest and northeast corners of Georgia to see highly successful enterprises. In the former there is Rock City, an extension into

Georgia of Tennessee's Lookout Mountain, which is perhaps the best-known private tourist attraction in North
America. "See Rock City" signs are so numerous that they
have been the subject of jokes by many well-known come-
dians, including that of one such sign being found painted
on a rock on the moon by an American astronaut. In the
latter, private developers have capitalized on the growing
number of skiing enthusiasts to develop Sky Valley as the
nation's southernmost ski slope. Also styled in the Alpine
tradition, it has an impressive lodge, chair lift and its own
snow-making machines to augment nature's lapses. It is so
remote in the northeast corner of Georgia that one must
drive into North Carolina to reach it. A grizzled mountaineer, Frank Rickman, designed the unique lodge by
drawing its plans on a paper sack.

Other North Georgia towns and communities are
capitalizing on their unique assets with festivals and fairs
to attract visitors and dollars and to promote the development of their areas. Notable among them are Blairsville's
Sorghum Festival, Clarkesville's Mountain Laurel Festival,
Clayton's Mountaineer Festival, Cleveland's Fall Leaf Festival, Dahlonega's Gold Rush Days and Fall Harvest Festival, Cornelia's Apple Harvest Fair, Lavonia's Annual Georgia State Bluegrass Music Festival, Toccoa's Spring Arts
Festival, and, perhaps the most unusual of all,
Chatsworth's Appalachian Wagon Train, which is a moving
exhibition of covered wagons, horses and other frontier-
type conveyances which travels over the mountains from
Chatsworth to Ellijay during the third week in July each
year. Wagon trains have always been popular in the mountains, and I have ridden on many of them.

The Sorghum Festival which I mentioned in an earlier
chapter features the famed Biscuit and Syrup Sopping
Contest, and Dahlonega's Gold Rush Days are planned to
tie into Dahlonega's wild and colorful history as the site of
the nation's first major gold discovery which touched off a
gold rush in 1828 before Mr. Sutter even thought of building his mill in California. With the advice and help of the

Tourist Division of the Georgia Department of Community Development, all of these promise to attain even greater significance and success in future years.

Mountain crafts by themselves attract many visitors. Virtually every town has at least one shop where authentic mountain products can be purchased, and some combine sales with actual demonstrations of the production of items like candles, homewoven cloth and pottery. Several of the more interesting and popular ones are the co-op run by Georgia Mountain Arts Products, Inc., inside the old train depot adjacent to the spectacular gorge over which Karl Wallenda made his daring tightwire walk at Tallulah Falls; the Mark of the Potter in an old grist mill on a remote mountain road near Batesville in Habersham County; Rabun Gap Crafts in Dillard which stocks hand-loomed articles; and the Craft Shop operated in conjunction with the impressive Berry Museum at Berry College near Rome, a college founded by the late Martha Berry and later financed by Henry Ford, Sr., to teach mountain children the skills of agriculture, homemaking and trades. No visitor to the North Georgia Highlands can get a complete picture of mountain life without visiting Berry College with its beautiful campus and inspiring history with roots in mountain heritage and history.

There are several renowned eating places in North Georgia which long have been *must* stops for those who wish to enjoy the delights of authentic mountain cooking. Both the Smith House in Dahlonega and the Dillard House in Dillard feature country cooking served family style with bowls of steaming vegetables and heaping platters of ham, fried chicken and other meats passed around as many times as desired. The apple butter at the Dillard House is a gourmet's treat. The Sautee Inn near Helen specializes in old-fashioned recipes served in buffet style, and one of the most colorful is Laprades Camp at the western end of Lake Burton in Rabun County. In keeping with true mountain hospitality, all of these eating places offer as many helpings as the visitor can put away and guarantee that no one ever leaves their tables hungry or not completely satisfied.

For those who wish the grandeur of mountain scenery, there is the vista of four states from the massive stone observation tower built on the crest of Brasstown Bald, Georgia's highest peak at 4,784 feet, by the U.S. Forest Service, which administers the 700,000 acre Chattahoochee National Forest covering parts of the 16 county area its heights command; the scenic drive along the Richard B. Russell Highway, which winds through 14 miles of the Forest's virgin mountain wilderness at elevations between 1,600 and 3,000 feet between Robertstown and Neel Gap; and visits to the overlooks along Tallulah Gorge in the northeast corner of Georgia; to 729-foot Amicalola Falls, Georgia's highest, in Dawson County in central North Georgia; and to 1,000-foot-deep Cloudland Canyon in the northwest corner of Georgia. Not far away from Amicalola Falls hikers can find the southern terminus of the Appalachian Trail at Springer Mountain and, for the more daring of the thrill-seekers who wish to emulate the derring-do of Burt Reynolds and company in the movie "Deliverance," entrance to the most hazardous whitewater stretch of the wild Chattooga River, which forms the northernmost boundary between Georgia and South Carolina, can be had from the Highway 76 Bridge eight miles east of Clayton. Many lives have been lost in the Chattooga by the unwary and the unprepared, and it is strongly recommended that no one try to navigate its lower reaches without proper equipment and an experienced guide.

History buffs can find much to fascinate them at New Echota, the restored village near Calhoun which once was the capital of the Cherokee Nation, the most advanced of the original Indian tribes of North America. The Cherokees had a tribal system of government modeled after our own federal government, and among the structures preserved is their Supreme Court building, which also doubled as a school, and the print shop with its original equipment which in 1828 began publication of the *Cherokee Phoenix,* a newspaper printed in the Cherokee language which was

created by the famed Sequoyah. To the north near Chatsworth is the Vann House, an outstanding example of Cherokee wealth and culture built in 1804 by James Vann. It is
constructed of brick produced in Vann's own kilns and
features classic cornices and hand carvings highlighting the
Cherokee Rose.

Students of Indian culture and the War Between the
States also find much to interest them in the area. For the
former there are the Etowah Indian Mounds located near
Cartersville on the site of the largest and most important
Indian settlement in the Etowah Valley during the period
1000 to 1500 A.D., and for the latter there is the Chicka-
mauga National Military Park, one of the oldest and largest
of the national military parks which was the site of one of
the South's last great victories.

For the lovers of water sports, boating and fishing,
there are the chains of beautiful lakes of cold, blue-green
waters fed by mountain rivers and streams formed by the
hydroelectric dams of the Georgia Power Company, the
Tennessee Valley Authority and the U.S. Army Corps of
Engineers as well as those built by the U.S. Forest Service
in the Chattahoochee National Forest. Among the most
scenic are those of the Georgia Power chain extending 38
miles along the Tugaloo and Tallulah Rivers beginning with
Lake Burton in the north to Lake Yonah in the south and
including Seed, Rabun, Tallulah and Tugaloo Lakes. The
largest are those of the Corps of Engineers, including the
mammoth Lake Sidney Lanier on the Chattahoochee
River, which had 15 million visitors in 1975, Lake Hart-
well on the Savannah River, Lake Allatoona on the
Etowah River and the newest, Carters Dam Lake on the
Coosawattee River which is one of the deepest and highest
in North America. Others include Lakes Conasauga,
Dockery, Blue Ridge, Nottley, Chatuge, Scott, Nancytown
and Russell.

And the hundreds of mountain streams offer a paradise
of opportunity for the trout fisherman. In fact, trout
fishing has become so popular that many private entrepre-

neurs have opened private trout-fishing ponds with guaranteed catches which have become very popular with tourists, much to the disdain of the purists among the fly fishermen.

Excellent camping facilities are available in the National Forest, along the shores of the lakes and in the State Parks dotted throughout the North Georgia region—Amicalola Falls at Juno, Black Rock Mountain at Mountain City, Cloudland Canyon at Trenton, Fort Mountain at Chatsworth, Moccasin Creek at Clayton, Red Top Mountain at Cartersville, and Vogel at Blairsville—as well as at the Unicoi Station near Helen.

Three unique attractions which claim much attention are the Gold Museum in Dahlonega housing exhibits commemorating the nation's first gold rush, the Moonshine Museum in Dawsonville featuring a collection of moonshine stills dating from 1800 and Traveler's Rest in Toccoa, one of the oldest buildings in Northeast Georgia which has served as a plantation house, a tavern, trading post and post office and is still intact with authentic furnishings. Don Carter has an excellent development at Skylake which features an authentic country drug store.

I have tried to the best of my knowledge and ability to be absolutely complete in cataloging the developments and attractions which characterize the Georgia Mountains today, and if any have been omitted it was an error of the head and not of the heart.

But of all the great things that have happened and are planned, all are dwarfed .into insignificance by the enduring grandeur of the mountains themselves. It is in them, adorned only as God Himself could create them, that my heart lies and where my ultimate ambition to spend my final days rests.

My thoughts in concluding this book are best expressed by the poem of unknown authorship, the first verse of which prefaces this chapter, and the others with which I conclude:

I would climb to brooding summits
With their old untarnished dreams,
Cool my heart in forest shadows
To the lull of falling streams.

I need the pure strong mornings,
When the soul of day is still,
With the touch of frost that kindles
The scarlet on the hill.

Lone trails and winding wood roads
To outlooks wild and high,
And the pale moon waiting sundown
Where ledges cut the sky.

My eyes dim for the skyline
Where purple peaks aspire
And the forges of the sunset
Flare up in golden fire.

Where cloud-mists from the warm earth
Roll up about their knees,
And hang their filmy tatters
Like prayers upon the trees.

# Afterword

Ten years have passed since I wrote this book and many things have changed during that decade. Shirley and I are proud grandparents now of a beautiful and sensitive granddaughter, Asia, 9, and a robust grandson, Justin Grady, 3, whose mother was recently killed in a tragic automobile accident.

No subject in the book received more attention than did my mother. Readers were fascinated with this remarkable woman, and rightly so. Birdie still lives or, more accurately, still breathes. This strong, vibrant woman, 92 years old September 1985, is in the Towns County Nursing Home in Hiawassee. Before allowing her to be placed there, we watched her body—and worse—her mind deteriorate. I came to see how heartbreaking and frightening seeing a loved one become senile can be.

My oldest son, Murphy is an attorney in Atlanta. My son, Matt is the general manager of a radio station I started in Young Harris in 1984. My beloved Aunt Phoebe died a few years ago and Shirley, always a good businesswoman and banker, is now the President of the Mountain Bank of Georgia in Hiawassee. Young Harris College will be 100 years old in 1986.

More and more people are discovering the beauty and solitude of the mountains and are coming to them in droves. Large trucks zoom by my front porch on the road where when I was a child we played hopscotch on the narrow pavement without being disturbed.

Changes. Changes all. But unchanging remains the serenity of my mountains and the strength I draw from them. Ten years older, wiser and slower I may be, the mountains are still within me. Thank God, they are still within me.

October 1985

171

# Index

172